Free Yourself from

EMETOPHOBIA

of related interest

Living with Emetophobia
Coping with Extreme Fear of Vomiting
Nicolette Heaton-Harris
Foreword by Linda Dean
ISBN 978 1 84310 536 7
eISBN 978 1 84642 629 2

Obsessive Compulsive Disorder Diary
A Self-Help Diary with CBT Activities
Charlotte Dennis
Foreword by Dr Amita Jassi and Dr Zoe Kindynis
ISBN 978 1 78775 053 1
eISBN 978 1 78775 054 8

The Anxiety Survival Guide
Getting through the Challenging Stuff
Bridie Gallagher, Sue Knowles and Phoebe McEwan
Illustrated by Emmeline Pidgen
ISBN 978 1 78592 641 9
eISBN 978 1 78592 642 6

We're all Mad Here
The No-Nonsense Guide to Living with Social Anxiety
Claire Eastham
Foreword by Natasha Devon MBE
ISBN 978 1 78592 082 0
eISBN 978 1 78450 343 7

Breaking Free from OCD
A CBT Guide for Young People and their Families
*Jo Derisley, Isobel Heyman, Sarah
Robinson and Cynthia Turner*
ISBN 978 1 84310 574 9
eISBN 978 1 84642 799 2

EMETOPHOBIA

A **CBT** Self-Help Guide for a Fear of Vomiting

Alexandra Keyes and David Veale

Jessica Kingsley Publishers
London and Philadelphia

First published in Great Britain in 2022 by Jessica Kingsley Publishers
An Hachette Company

8

Copyright © Alexandra Keyes and David Veale 2022

Disclaimer: The information contained in this book is not intended to replace the
services of trained medical professionals or to be a substitute for medical advice.
You are advised to consult a doctor on any matters relating to your health, and
in particular on any matters that may require diagnosis or medical attention.

A CIP catalogue record for this title is available from the
British Library and the Library of Congress

ISBN 978 1 78775 331 0
eISBN 978 1 78775 332 7

Printed and bound in Great Britain by Bell & Bain Limited

Jessica Kingsley Publishers' policy is to use papers that are natural,
renewable and recyclable products and made from wood grown in sus-
tainable forests. The logging and manufacturing processes are expected to
conform to the environmental regulations of the country of origin.

Jessica Kingsley Publishers
Carmelite House
50 Victoria Embankment
London EC4Y 0DZ

www.jkp.com

Contents

Acknowledgements

We would like to acknowledge all the people with emetophobia whom we have treated and included in our research. We would also like to thank all the people with emetophobia and the clinicians who have given their valuable time and feedback to help us with this book. You have all contributed to our understanding of this complex and difficult-to-treat condition. You are the inspiration in making this work accessible so that more people with emetophobia can reach meaningful goals and live a life without fear.

Please note that the worksheets marked with ✳ are available to download and print from https://library.jkp.com/redeem using the voucher code NTDVBZX.

> **Trigger warning:** In this book, we use words to describe emetophobia that may be upsetting for people with the condition.

CHAPTER 1

What is Emetophobia?

Introduction

In this book, we hope to describe the experience of living with emetophobia, what keeps it going, and how to overcome it. We aim to set out a structured and easy-to-follow plan for facing your fear that will allow you to live your life in the way that you want to. This is a plan you might do with the support of a loved one or with the help of a therapist.

We want to acknowledge first that emetophobia is a difficult problem to live with and to solve. However, we have successfully treated many people with the condition, and with the right tools and attitude it is absolutely possible to achieve your goals. We know that this can seem like a daunting prospect to begin with, as emetophobia can make you feel extremely fearful, and can cause you to miss out on many things that you value in life. People with a phobia of vomiting often end up avoiding lots of activities that they value and enjoy, or avoiding others that they love in order to keep themselves 'safe' from vomiting. We know that it can be a very serious condition that has a big impact on the quality of your life. It can often seem too daunting to think about making changes to these behaviours and to move forward. However, it is important to know that you are not alone. There are many people, like you, who have the same overwhelming thoughts and emotions, for whom being sick or seeing others vomit seems like a fate worse than death.

We also want to overcome some of the stigma surrounding emetophobia. It is often misunderstood (even by health professionals), and people without emetophobia may regard it as trivial. We know it's not like other specific phobias of, say, spiders. Many of our patients have said if they had the choice, they would choose to die rather than vomit. They live in constant fear of not knowing if norovirus or another illness is about to be transmitted to them and cause them to vomit.

From working with many people with emetophobia and from researching the condition over many years, we know that even though it can be hard to overcome, it is very possible to do so. We know many people who have shown extraordinary acts of courage in order to face their fears and beat their emetophobia. We have worked with them to turn their phobia into a 'fear' of vomiting, which is easier to live with. This is important because we acknowledge that not everyone can be 'cured' of emetophobia, but they are able to recover the parts of their lives that they feel they have missed out on. They may still have some fears of vomiting but no longer feel restricted and have told us that they feel more able to enjoy what matters to them: working in a rewarding job or reaching their potential at school or in college; eating the foods they enjoy; going to the places that interest them; caring for loved ones; relaxing around alcohol, or loosening the rules around cleaning and hygiene. They are able to spend time doing what is meaningful, instead of always trying to follow the rules that fear sets out for them and which take them away from what really matters. It often takes a huge leap of faith to take the first steps, but we know that the end result is worth it. We hope that this book will help you to begin that journey.

Please note, if you are reading this book during a pandemic, some of the tasks such as being close to others may be against government guidelines. However, if the pandemic is over and life has returned to normal, then it is important to learn how to tolerate your distress and to test out whether your findings best fit the theory that you have a problem of worrying about vomiting to solve (not a problem of vomiting itself).

How to use this book

We have included lots of practical tips on how to overcome your emetophobia in this book. You might be tempted to skip straight to the later chapters to find out how you can start to make changes. However, we recommend that you start the book from the beginning and read the chapters through in order. This is because we find that a good understanding of your problems and how they are maintained helps you to know exactly what needs to change.

We have also included spaces for you to reflect on your own personal experiences, and to help develop your understanding of key ideas throughout the book. We find that the more time you take to complete the exercises, the more you will get out of the chapters and the information provided. The worksheets marked with ✳ are available to download and print from https://library. jkp.com/redeem using the voucher code NTDVBZX.

Lastly, we have used characters throughout the book to help explain ideas and to apply them to real life. These characters are based on real people with emetophobia whom we have worked with, although names and details have been changed to protect their identities. Although we have tried to choose real-life examples that represent a range of features of emetophobia, we acknowledge that every person's experience of the condition will be unique to them. You might struggle with entirely different aspects of emetophobia from those reflected in our characters. This does not mean that you are alone in your own experience of emetophobia, or that you cannot follow the same set of principles outlined in the book.

Sally

Sally, aged 26, had been afraid of vomiting since she was eight years old when she saw a classmate being sick at school. Ever since this episode, she had been very afraid that she would be sick herself and that the vomiting would be awful and she would be unable to stop. Sally often felt very nauseous and worried that she could therefore be sick at any moment. In order to manage her nausea and fear, she avoided eating foods she thought were unsafe, such as chicken or seafood, and did not eat at restaurants or friends' houses. She ate a very restricted diet and had lost a lot of weight. She also avoided contact with ill people or children who might vomit. She washed her hands excessively and avoided enclosed spaces, such as travel on public transport. Sally often checked for signs of danger in her environment and frequently sought reassurance from friends and family that she would not vomit. They were becoming very fed up with her. She scanned her body for evidence of nausea or being unwell and took small sips of water and chewed mints to manage any unpleasant physical sensations.

Jon

Jon was in his 40s and remembered being very scared of vomiting for many years. He recalled being sick in the car when he was a young boy, and his parents responding angrily. This made him feel very afraid and ashamed at that time. He had become extremely preoccupied with the idea of catching an illness such as norovirus that would make him vomit, and believed that vomiting would be violent and catastrophic, and would last several days. He therefore avoided any possible crowds and many public places, especially during winter. He also avoided hospitals, and socializing with people who were potentially ill. He had spent hours researching viral outbreaks on the internet. He avoided touching surfaces and sharing food with others. Jon really wanted to travel, but his fear of becoming ill and vomiting prevented him from going abroad. His life was very restricted, and his mood had deteriorated.

Anna

Anna was 35 years old and developed a fear of vomiting at university. She remembered being ill with food poisoning, and ever since she had feared becoming unwell again, or other people being sick near her. She had a two-year-old son and was very nervous about him being sick and then becoming unwell herself. She believed that she would not be able to cope and that her vomiting would go on forever. In order to manage this, she did not let her son eat risky foods, and did not let him play anywhere dirty or with other sick children. She rarely left home and was becoming isolated from friends and family. Anna spent hours cleaning surfaces with anti-bacterial wipes in her home. She restricted her own food to small amounts and was underweight. She did not eat out where she was not able to cook the food herself. Her partner complained that their food was often charred or overcooked. She was constantly monitoring her stomach and whether it was safe to eat. Anna and her husband would love a second child, but she was avoiding a second pregnancy due to concerns about her vomiting in pregnancy and her son becoming unwell. Also, Anna engaged in mental rituals to keep herself and her family safe. She counted to certain numbers, and repeated certain words and phrases over and over in her head when she feared they might become ill. She touched wood and avoided stepping on the cracks in the pavement to reduce the likelihood of her son vomiting when she was away from home.

Sally, Jon and Anna were all experiencing emetophobia, an intense fear of vomiting. We will outline the typical features of emetophobia and what it might look like below.

Vomiting of self or others?

People with emetophobia are most often afraid of vomiting themselves, and, to a lesser extent, of someone else vomiting. This is usually because they believe they could catch something, and they will be sick as a result. Thus, some people can cope better with a person who is drunk if they know they are not contagious. They may still find someone else vomiting difficult because it reminds them of past experiences of vomiting, or that they could vomit one day. There are some people who are only fearful of others vomiting (and not really themselves) but this is much less common.

Intrusive images

People with emetophobia often experience intrusive images of their self or others vomiting. These are unwanted pictures or sensations of worst-case scenarios that pop up uninvited and are beyond a person's control or conscious thought. These can be experienced in the first-person perspective looking out (e.g. an image of yourself vomiting in a horrible way), in a specific situation, or as other people's reactions. They can also be experienced as an observer, for example watching yourself vomit in a frightening scenario, or observing someone else vomit in front of you. These images are likely to cause much distress and feelings of anxiety and can even make physical sensations of nausea worse. The pictures can be 'flashbacks' – a reminder of a past experience of vomiting – and can feel very real, as if you are living it again. They can also be 'flashforwards' where you imagine vomiting in the future. It is also common for people with emetophobia to experience their fears in other ways as well as pictures, such as intrusive smells, tastes or physical sensations like feeling sick. These experiences can occur in any of the senses and can be just as frightening as a picture popping into your head.

People can experience distressing imagery in the form of nightmares about themselves or others vomiting. Nightmares can feel very real and scary to the person experiencing them. They can even lead to avoidance of sleep or trouble going back to sleep. Nightmares can often be related to past traumatic experiences of vomiting. If this is the case, then people might need help to emotionally process the memories that they relate to. We talk more about how to work with distressing images in Chapter 5.

Physical sensations

Most people with emetophobia experience sensations of nausea or discomfort in their body, usually their stomach, when they are anxious, and these make them think they are going to vomit. These sensations can include a bloated feeling or stomach pain. They are very real, and it can be unhelpful when people suggest that they are imagined or 'in the head'. As real as they are, they can often be caused by feelings of anxiety, and then misinterpreted as direct evidence that vomiting is more likely. Other physical sensations of anxiety can include a racing heart or heart palpitations, sweating and cold flushes, a churning stomach, diarrhoea, tingling hands and feet and breathlessness. These are all very normal physical responses to the emotion of panic, and do not mean that anything catastrophic is about to happen. Panic attacks in anticipation of vomiting are therefore very common in emetophobia.

Thoughts of vomiting

When people with emetophobia experience nausea or other physical sensations, it is common for their minds to jump to the worst and most scary thing to happen. In this case, it is being sick, and usually in a dramatic or horrible way. The worst thing might also be losing control of themselves or their body or that the feelings of being out of control will go on forever and ever. They may fear being unable to get back control. A key issue is not being able to tolerate uncertainty so that not knowing whether they are going to be sick may be worse than knowing they are going to be sick at a particular time. Sometimes, people have specific fears about vomiting such as they might choke or die or the vomiting will carry on forever.

People might be more afraid to vomit in front of others because they are fearful of being judged by others or that others will not want to know them or will find them repulsive. When the fear of vomiting is focused only on what others think about them vomiting (and is not so anxiety provoking if they are alone), then it becomes more of a social phobia, which we describe below. This is much less common.

Specific situations often trigger thoughts, such as being in a confined space where it is less easy to escape. Often vomiting is seen as 100 per cent awful. In many cases, a person with emetophobia will be unable to explain why the idea of vomiting is so awful, they just know that it is to be avoided at all costs. This is why any therapy that tries to help you to be 'rational', gives lots of coping statements or tries to teach mindfulness meditation is bound to fail.

Worry

In emetophobia, it is very common to spend lots of time worrying about vomiting. You might spend a lot of time mentally planning how to avoid being sick, how to escape a situation, or how to cope in a worst-case scenario. These worries can often start with 'what if'; for example, 'What if my child is sick away from home and I won't know what to do?', 'What if I am sick in the meeting in front of all my colleagues?', 'What if someone is sick on me and makes me ill?' Worries often take the form of being the absolute worst-case scenario of what might happen.

Sometimes people can have positive beliefs about the benefits of worry: 'If I worry about this then I can stop myself from vomiting' or, 'If I worry then I can prepare myself in case it happens.' This can make the person feel more certain or prepared in the short term, and therefore temporarily reduces their anxiety. However, there are often negative consequences to worrying, including increasing overall anxiety and preoccupation with the problem. It can make vomiting seem even more awful if so much mental energy is going into stopping it from happening (and when you learn that you have no control over whether you vomit or not).

Attention

When we are very afraid of something happening, it is common for shifts in our attention to occur. This is helpful when there is an actual threat, such as a lion or a mugger, and you need to be focused in order to be alert and prepared to fight or take flight. In the case of emetophobia, attention can shift inwards and become very self-focused. For example, people can spend many hours scanning their body for any signs or symptoms that vomiting might be imminent. Attention might also shift outwards, for example watching closely for other people who might be sick, or looking for escape routes or people who could help if the worst does in fact happen. As you can imagine, being on constant alert can have many unintended consequences, and make you believe there is a threat of you vomiting at any moment. It is also extremely tiring.

Avoidance

People with emetophobia spend a lot of time worrying about vomiting. This makes them try to avoid things that might make them more likely to vomit or activities that make them feel sick. For example, they might stop eating certain foods that carry more risk of food poisoning, like seafood or meat. We discuss some of the differences between emetophobia with disordered eating and anorexia nervosa below. People with emetophobia may not eat in places where they cannot cook the food themselves. They might try to avoid eating in restaurants or buffets that are seen as 'unclean' or because they cannot cook the food themselves. Travelling to foreign countries and eating foreign foods is often seen as very unsafe by someone with emetophobia. Travel on public transport, boats and planes is also often avoided as they can't 'escape' easily. They might also want to avoid public toilets, pubs, hospitals, visiting their GP's surgery and places with lots of children. People with emetophobia might avoid drinking or taking drugs themselves in case they vomit (rather than for moral or other reasons). They avoid certain media when there might be references to vomiting. They might avoid certain words relating to vomiting and use euphemisms like 'feeling unwell'. Often people with emetophobia find it very hard to visit unwell relatives in hospital, or to care for loved ones when they are sick. This can make them feel very guilty and ashamed. In some very sad cases, people avoid having general anaesthetic or women avoid getting pregnant or even end a pregnancy for fear of vomiting.

Safety-seeking behaviours

When people are very afraid of being sick, it is natural that they use strategies or behaviours to help them, in their view, to reduce the likelihood of this happening. These are called *safety-seeking behaviours* because they help the person to feel safer against vomiting. There are many examples of these in emetophobia. People might excessively check the expiry dates on food or overcook their food. They might also have 'eating rituals' like only eating a certain amount of food at certain times using the same plate or utensils. They might suck on mints, chew gum or sip water to make themselves feel less sick. They might wash their hands a lot or clean surfaces at home very often. Often, people with emetophobia check their health and how they feel, and other people's health. They might frequently ask their loved ones if they feel ill or sick. It is common for people to reassure themselves a lot by telling themselves they feel okay or that they won't be sick. They will often ask their loved ones to tell them they are okay as well. We discuss this in more detail below in relation to symptoms of obsessive compulsive disorder.

Impact on quality of life

Emetophobia can have a very serious impact on a person's quality of life. It can affect their ability to live their life in the way that they want to. Living with emetophobia can make it very hard to make and keep friends and romantic relationships. It can make it hard to be around family or other loved ones. You might find you spend lots of time alone as it feels hard to join in because of your fear. People with emetophobia can also find that their family life is affected if women are scared of pregnancy or parents find it hard to care for their children. It can mean that you find it hard to reach your full potential at work, school or college. This is because it can be difficult to concentrate when you are very worried about vomiting. It might also be hard to be around work or schoolmates. You might find it hard to do things you are interested in like travelling, going to new places, exercising or being in crowded places like the cinema, theatres and shopping centres. Lastly, it can have a significant impact on your physical health, for example if you have a restricted diet and are becoming malnourished and underweight.

Emetophobia is different from other phobias. Feeling sick and vomiting are experiences that are difficult to escape and avoid. As an example, if you are afraid of dogs or spiders, then it might be easier to avoid them and to treat this by facing up to your fears. However, emetophobia can impact more areas of people's lives as internal experiences are much more difficult to avoid than other things. Therefore, it can be very hard living with emetophobia, and the impact on day-to-day life can be very severe for some people.

Making a diagnosis of specific phobia

Only a trained professional can tell you whether you have

emetophobia or not. The accepted term in the World Health Organization's International Classification of Diseases is a specific 'phobia'. There are many different types of specific phobias, for example animals (e.g. dogs, spiders, mice, insects), blood and injury (e.g. needles, injections), natural environment (e.g. heights, weather, darkness, water), situational (e.g. enclosed spaces, flying on a plane, trains) and lastly what is termed 'others' (e.g. vomiting, choking or incontinence). So emetophobia is just one of many specific phobias. However, we know that emetophobia is different from and more limiting than other specific phobias. The questions listed below might be used by a health professional to diagnose a specific phobia of vomiting.

Do you have emetophobia?

1. Do you experience a marked fear of vomiting?

2. Does experiencing a trigger related to vomiting make you feel anxious or panicky?

3. Do you recognize that your fear of vomiting is excessive or out of all proportion to the danger of vomiting?

4. Do you avoid situations that could result in vomiting or do you endure them with intense anxiety?

5. Has your fear of vomiting persisted for at least six months?

6. Does your fear of vomiting cause you great distress? Does it interfere in areas of your life such as relationships, health, family, work or school, or your social life?

How common is emetophobia?

Specific phobias in general are extremely common, with about seven per cent of people in the community reporting a phobia.[1] However, while emetophobia is rare compared to other types of specific phobias, such as phobia of animals or insects, heights, blood or needles, observations within our clinic suggests that it is the most common specific phobia in people seeking treatment for a phobia.

Research also suggests that emetophobia occurs more frequently in women. Thus at least 90 per cent of people with emetophobia are women, and it may be helpful to think about why this is. Differences in the way women report anxieties might explain why more women are found to have emetophobia. Men may be more ashamed to admit fears of vomiting, and therefore their phobia could go undetected. Differences in sex hormones and genetics may also make women more vulnerable to developing emetophobia compared to men. Not enough is known at present about gender differences in emetophobia, though these differences are much more marked than we see in other specific phobias. There may be a genetic influence that makes women more vulnerable to developing emetophobia. There is some evidence that women may be more prone to the feeling of disgust. Men are more likely than women to regard vomiting as something funny (after a heavy bout of drinking, 'better out than in') rather than revolting. Women are generally more hygienic than men and more likely to develop contamination fears in obsessive compulsive disorder (OCD); however, the gender difference is still greater in emetophobia than OCD.

---

1   Wardenaar, K.J., Lim, C.C.W., Al-Hamzawi, A.O., Alonso, J. et al. (2017). 'The cross-national epidemiology of specific phobia in the World Mental Health Surveys.' *Psychological Medicine*, 47(10), 1744–1760. doi:10.1017/S0033291717000174.

Emetophobia usually develops in childhood or adolescence but commonly presents up to ten years later in young adults. As far as we know, it occurs in people of all races and across all backgrounds.

Differences between a fear of vomiting and emetophobia

Well, most people hate vomiting, don't they? Yes, it is true that vomiting can be unpleasant and that vomit itself can trigger feelings of fear and disgust in most people. From an evolutionary perspective, it makes sense that vomiting and vomit itself are unpleasant, in order to keep us safe from illness and disease. However, a dislike or fear of vomiting *is not the same* as emetophobia. A fear of vomiting is relatively common and may be experienced by many people, whereas emetophobia is rarer. Emetophobia is likely to result in extreme anxiety and distress, avoidance of many day-to-day activities, and changes in behaviour and attention. It can have a very detrimental effect on a person's quality of life. It is likely that emetophobia will require treatment for that person to be able to live their life in the way that is important to them. People with emetophobia need support to engage in valued goals and activities that are being avoided.

Overlap and differences between emetophobia and other disorders

Do I have emetophobia or OCD?

If you have emetophobia you might have been given a diagnosis of OCD. This is because there are many similarities between the two. Everyone is different but we think there is a *continuum* between emetophobia and OCD. At one end of the spectrum, 'pure' emetophobia is like other specific phobias. The main feature is being highly avoidant of vomiting and of situations and activities that may increase the risk of vomiting. At the OCD end of the spectrum, the difficulty is with uncertainty about whether you or someone else is going to vomit, and involves many repetitive behaviours. Such people just want to know for certain if and when they are going to vomit or how long it will last for. Individuals have difficulty tolerating not knowing whether they might be sick or not. There may be magical thinking (e.g the idea that if you think or wish yourself to vomit or do not carry out a ritual, it will make you vomit). There is more compulsive washing and other repetitive behaviours that aim to stop vomiting. There may be other symptoms of OCD, for example intrusive unacceptable thoughts or images or wanting order and symmetry in one's belongings.

Research shows that in a sample of people with emetophobia, the majority either often or always show repetitive behaviours. These include checking sell-by dates, checking others to see if they are unwell, excessive hand washing or washing children's hands, rituals or counting to stop vomiting (e.g. touching wood, doing things to a specific number), reassuring themselves or seeking reassurance from others. Many of these behaviours are *similar* to OCD; however, all have the intention of monitoring whether one is going to vomit or stopping vomiting. There is no doubt there are similar processes in emetophobia and OCD, and it may be more important to focus on these rather than worry about whether it's called emetophobia or OCD.

People at the OCD end of the spectrum are more likely to express magical or superstitious thinking. Understanding the problem as OCD may be important, as therapy will need to focus more on difficulties with uncertainty as the main problem. All these checking and washing behaviours need to be stopped and we will discuss how to do this in Chapter 5. Sometimes medication may be helpful at the OCD end of the spectrum, and we discuss this in Chapter 8.

Do I have an eating disorder?

Emetophobia sometimes gets confused with anorexia nervosa, which is an eating disorder involving low weight, food restriction and fear of gaining weight. This is because sometimes people with emetophobia are so fearful of vomiting that they restrict the amount of food they eat, so that they become underweight and malnourished. Such individuals may become very low in their weight and may be seen in an eating disorders service in order to regain a healthy weight. Such individuals often feel very mis-understood in an eating disorders service. People with anorexia nervosa are motivated to restrict their eating in order to keep control and are driven by a fear of gaining weight. They may be proud of their ability to control their hunger and of the weight they have lost. However, someone with emetophobia usually wants a healthy weight and would like to eat normally. They may be fed up with being treated as if they have anorexia. Of course, if you are underweight and malnourished, it is important to increase your weight (e.g. initially by nutritional supplements) as other-wise your thinking may be very rigid, and it is more difficult to overcome your phobia.

There are three main ways that emetophobia might lead you to restrict your food.

1. You reduce the amount of food as you think there is less to vomit. A restricted amount may lead to feeling 'full', as you

think that eating more increases your risk of vomiting. This is in fact not true – you would have to eat a *massive* amount of food to vomit. Think Mr Creosote in Monty Python's *The Meaning of Life* (this film is not of course for people with emetophobia, but you may have heard about it).

2. You restrict food in certain contexts, for example avoiding eating food cooked by someone else or in a salad bar, buffet or restaurant. This may be due to having less control over the preparation of the food, which increases the perceived risk of vomiting.

3. You avoid certain types of food, such as seafood, which might have a slightly higher risk for vomiting. Foods associated with past experiences of vomiting may be avoided because of their association. A variation of this is restriction to a narrow range of foods that are regarded as 'safe' as they are not associated with vomiting (e.g. eating only two or three things bought from the same supermarket). This is similar to 'magical thinking'.

Research[2] shows that in a group of people with emetophobia, only a small number had a very low weight and this might be confused with anorexia. The most common behaviours around food were avoiding food that was cooked or prepared by someone else (e.g. salad bars and buffets); avoiding foreign meals or pre-cooked foods; restricting seafood or meat; excessively checking sell-by dates and the freshness of food; cooking food for a long time or burning food; and rituals around eating that may stop vomiting. Restricting the

---

2   Veale, D., Costa, A., Murphy, P. and Ellison, N. (2012). 'Abnormal eating behaviour in people with a specific phobia of vomiting (emetophobia).' *European Eating Disorders Review*, 20, 414–418. https://dx.doi.org/10.1002/erv.1159.

amount or types of food is linked to more severe symptoms of emetophobia and disability.

So, in conclusion, many people with emetophobia may have disordered eating or abnormal eating behaviours. This does not mean you have an eating disorder like anorexia. Yes, the disordered eating needs to be a target in therapy but as part of the treatment for emetophobia. This means focusing on the fear of vomiting and past experiences of vomiting. It means targeting all the situations and types of food you avoid and activities you feel you have to repeat.

Emetophobia and social anxiety

Research has found an overlap between the symptoms of emetophobia and social anxiety. Social anxiety is a disorder whereby people avoid social situations for fear of saying or doing something wrong that will lead to being judged or rejected by others. Approximately one to two out of ten people with symptoms of emetophobia also report symptoms of social anxiety. This may be especially common in individuals who fear vomiting in front of others for fear of negative judgement, or being laughed or shouted at. There may be similarities in avoidance behaviours between those with emetophobia and those with social anxiety. For example, those who fear vomiting in social situations may be more likely to avoid them in the same way that people with social anxiety would. However, the main difference between emetophobia and social anxiety is the nature of the fears. In emetophobia, the person most likely fears the vomiting itself. People who are socially anxious will worry that there is something they might say or do in front of others that will cause negative judgement. The fear is much more in relation to things that can go wrong when interacting with others and being rejected by them as a result. Even though there may be an overlap, it is important to know whether there is a clear distinction between the two so that the right treatment can be offered.

Emetophobia and health anxiety

Health anxiety is an anxiety disorder that causes people to believe that they have an undiagnosed and usually terminal illness. This belief leads to excessive worry, self-monitoring of body symptoms, and avoidance. The symptoms of emetophobia may be similar to those of health anxiety. For example, people with emetophobia may spend time worrying about becoming ill and contaminated with a toxin that could make them vomit. They may excessively check their body for signs of illness or ask others for reassurance that they are not ill. People with emetophobia might avoid other sick people or hospitals for fear of becoming contaminated. They might also spend time researching illnesses online. The main difference between emetophobia and health anxiety is the fear being reported. In emetophobia, it is most likely to be a fear of illnesses *that will cause vomiting only*. People with health anxiety tend to fear any serious illness that may not necessarily cause vomiting. If you are worried about getting ill generally or that you have a serious illness such as cancer that the doctors have missed, then it is more likely that you suffer from health anxiety. It will be important to make this distinction so that you can find the right resources to help you.

Emetophobia and panic disorder

Panic disorder is an anxiety disorder involving the experience of frequent panic attacks. Everyone will experience panic and anxiety at times, as this is a normal response to threat. However, people with panic disorder will experience frequent panic attacks involving an intense feeling of anxiety that is accompanied by physical sensations such as a racing heartbeat, feeling faint, sweating, nausea, difficulty breathing and chest pains. These are the most common physical symptoms, but there are many more that can be felt during a panic attack. The person usually misinterprets these symptoms as a sign that something very scary is about to happen, such as fainting, choking, heart attack or even death. Panic attacks can lead to severe anxiety and avoidance of many activities. There is often an overlap between emetophobia and panic disorder, as people with emetophobia can experience panic attacks when they are very frightened of feeling sick or vomiting. However, the main difference between panic disorder and emetophobia is that the panic attacks in panic disorder will most often happen *out of the blue and for no reason*, whereas in emetophobia, panic attacks will be triggered by fears of vomiting. If you experience panic attacks as part of your emetophobia, then it will be helpful to include panic attacks in your understanding of how your difficulties are being maintained. If your experience of panic attacks is severe, then it might be that you need some help with those first before starting work on your emetophobia.

Emetophobia and depression

If your emetophobia is very severe and you miss out on many things in life such as relationships, education, career and social life, you may have developed a depression which is secondary to your emetophobia. In other words, if you did not have emetophobia then you are unlikely to have developed depression. You may have become very down in your mood and unable to enjoy any of the normal pleasures in life. You may be thinking excessively and be very negative about yourself and the future. You lack any motivation, are inactive, and your sleep is disturbed. These are all classic symptoms of depression, which will need to be treated alongside your emetophobia.

Chapter summary

- Emetophobia is a severe phobia of vomiting, either yourself vomiting or seeing other people vomit.
- Research shows that emetophobia is the most common problem in people seeking treatment for a specific phobia.
- Common features of emetophobia include nausea, intrusive thoughts and images about vomiting, avoidance of feared situations and activities related to vomiting, worry, self-focused attention and behaviours designed to keep you safe.
- Emetophobia can lead to a huge reduction in quality of life and is *not* the same as being afraid of vomiting.
- Emetophobia can look similar to other mental health problems such as an eating disorder, OCD, social anxiety, health anxiety and panic disorder.
- It is important to see a mental health professional if you are unsure if this is the right description of your difficulties.

———

CHAPTER 2

Causes of Emetophobia and What Keeps it Going

What causes emetophobia?

It is still unclear what exactly causes a person to develop eme-tophobia. We need more research to develop better treatments. However, what we do know is that there may be several factors that contribute to emetophobia. Often it is a mixture of factors as opposed to one single reason or event that leads someone to fear vomiting. These can include early life experiences, factors in a person's environment, personality or psychological traits, and biological or genetic factors.

We also know that it is never a person's fault and you are never to blame for having emetophobia. You have no control over your genes or the traits that affect the way you think and feel. None of us is able to choose the early experiences, or environment, that are so important in shaping who we are. You cannot be responsible for how these things come together to make life difficult. Anybody who lives through hardship can be more vulnerable to developing anxieties and phobias, and it is important to be encouraging and kind to yourself when trying to understand how these problems have developed. We will outline the main factors that lead to developing emetophobia below, but remember it can be one or a combination of a number of these.

Basic emotions in emetophobia

Before we help you to gain an understanding of your emetophobia, it's important to consider how evolution has affected the way our minds work. All of us have what could be called a 'design fault' in the brain. Evidence shows that a part of our brain is similar to reptiles and mammals and we call this the 'old brain'. It is responsible for our basic emotions and drives that help us to stay safe, to find food and to reproduce. We also have a 'new brain' that is well developed and is responsible for enabling us to do more advanced tasks. These include solving problems, being creative, using language, planning and being rational. In order to fully understand the motivation behind our behaviour, we need to look at how the new brain relates to the old brain.

There are three main systems in our 'old brain':

1. The 'threat' system. This helps us to stay tuned to noticing and responding to threats in our environment and in our lives. It allows us to feel anxious, as well as anger and disgust, in order to detect threat, and it helps us to respond by 'fight, flight or freeze'. The threat system has become too sensitive in emetophobia.
2. The 'drive' system. This motivates us to seek out and take pleasure from finding important resources such as food, relationships, sex and approval from others. This drive helps us to

survive, to be more likely to find a mate and reproduce, and to experience pleasure and excitement. Sometimes, people with emetophobia try to cope by doing lots and keeping busy, which is achieved by the drive system. However, it is common that the drive system gets overwhelmed by the threat system, which may cause feelings of depression and lack of motivation or drive.

3. The 'compassion' system. This allows us to form relationships with others and to understand ourselves, and gives us a sense of well-being and contentment. The threat system may also overwhelm this system in emetophobia, making it hard to self-soothe and connect with others. Psychologist Paul Gilbert and his colleagues use compassion-focused therapy to help people to develop self-compassion. These techniques balance out both the threat and drive systems, which may be causing problems if either becomes overly dominant. This is important because we know that facing up to your fears is more successful if you can be compassionate. This is the ability to be kind, caring, understanding, tolerate distress, be non-judgemental and encouraged to approach difficult situations. The compassion may come from yourself or from another person.

Anxiety

An important skill is to be able to recognize and label different emotions. Let's now look at how the threat system works in emetophobia. In order to understand what causes anxiety, we need to go back many thousands of years to the time of the primitive man and woman. Back then there were plenty of external threats, such as the sabretooth tiger looking for dinner. The threat system was very important in being alert to this danger. As soon as the primitive man or woman saw the tiger, their threat system would have caused them to feel anxiety and panic. This would have auto-matically prepared their body to either *fight* the tiger, to *freeze* or to *flee*. So, this system must work very quickly in order to keep a person safe from harm and help us to survive.

In emetophobia and other anxiety disorders, threats are not external in the environment (like a hungry tiger). They are internal, or in the mind (i.e. the idea of having norovirus or being sick). These threats are made by our 'new brains' which make it possible to imagine threat like disease or getting ill, even if it is not as probable as the threat from a hungry tiger standing in front of us. So, the way our 'new' brain and 'old' brain interact with each other can cause problems. The new brain is rational and tries to tell the old brain that something is safe and not contaminated by norovirus. However, the old brain threat system is designed to act quickly, it does not have time to weigh things up when keeping us safe from danger. So, an internal threat automatically activates the fight or flight system in just the same way as a real external threat would.

It can sometimes feel as if you have two parts to your mind – an anxious emetophobia part and a calm rational part – and this is why. The difficulty is that the threat system is designed to 'trump' any other system in order to survive. Anxiety is a sign that your threat system is creating a normal response, just to something that is not dangerous. Unfortunately, you can't just stop this 'fight or flight' response or get rid of it. It's part of your normal survival mechanism. However, learning more about what activates your threat system, how it responds and what you can do that makes it worse or better will help.

Disgust

As well as an anxious response to nausea and the thought of

vomiting, the emotion of disgust plays an important role in emetophobia. It is a common and universal response to feel disgust at vomiting or the sight, sound or smell of vomit. However, people with emetophobia may experience a more extreme disgust response to vomit and vomiting. For example, research[1] suggests that people with emetophobia experience disgust more quickly, and think more negatively about disgust experiences, than people without emetophobia. Individuals with emetophobia are also more likely to use the feeling of disgust as evidence of danger, risk of contamination and becoming ill. Not only does this suggest that disgust may be involved in developing emetophobia, it may also contribute to the severe aversion to and avoidance of vomiting, which is likely to make the condition worse. Therefore, the emotional responses experienced in emetophobia can be more complex than a pure fear response. It can be helpful to understand the role that disgust plays in your own experience of emetophobia as a first step to overcoming it. It's also worth acknowledging that tolerating the feeling of disgust is tricky.

Anger and shame

Anger is part of the fight response to a threat. It can sometimes play a part in emetophobia. For example, you may become angry if someone has triggered you or done something to put you at a perceived risk of vomiting. More commonly the anger is directed at yourself for avoiding something that you wanted to do. Here the problem is more one of shame. This is like an internal bully judging you for being 'pathetic' for being afraid of vomiting and

---

1   Van Overveld, M., de Jong, P.J., Peters, M.L., van Hout, W.J.P.J. and Bourman, T.K. (2008). 'An internet-based study on the relation between disgust sensitivity and emetophobia.' *Journal of Anxiety Disorders*, 22(3), 524–531. https://doi.org/10.1016/j.janxdis.2007.04.001.

demanding you pull yourself together. You may also feel that when you were younger your carers were critical or humiliated you for vomiting in the wrong place or at the wrong time. These memories may persist so that you may feel that others are still critical or judgemental. Shame for having emetophobia may now interfere in your recovery, so it's important to identify and tackle this emotion during therapy. This will enable you to become understanding, kind and encouraging, and to learn to tolerate the distress and approach difficult problems. As we discussed above, it's not your fault that you vomited as a child or now have emetophobia – others can now help you recover but you will have to take the lead.

Early life experiences

Some people may go on to develop emetophobia after a troubling experience of vomiting when they are young. It is difficult to prove this as someone with emetophobia tries to look for reasons why they have emetophobia. Therefore, we don't really know if people without emetophobia might have had similar experiences. Some people will be affected by early experiences of vomiting, and for some vulnerable young people it can mean they start to fear vomit. This can be either vomiting themselves or seeing another person vomit. It is common during these experiences that people think about vomiting in an anxious way. For example, the person may think that they are going to die or be severely harmed when they vomit. These thoughts then lead them to fear another episode of vomiting in the future.

Other people's reactions to episodes of vomiting can also be very important. A person might believe they were abandoned by others after vomiting. They might remember feeling really embarrassed about vomiting in a public place in front of other people.

They might think that other people judged them at the time for being sick, when this is actually not the case. In some cases, they might have wrongly been made to feel ashamed of being sick. Some people report being laughed at for it. Other people might have unfairly reacted with disgust to that person being sick in front of them. Even though this may be understandable, it can be hugely unhelpful for the person who was sick. Often this is wrongly interpreted as people finding them *as a person* disgusting instead of the vomiting itself. When people think about an event in a negative way like this, it is likely to cause strong negative emotions at the time, such as fear, anxiety and shame.

People often report feeling very scared at the time of being sick. It may have come on very suddenly, and they may not have known why it was happening or when it would end. Perhaps they did not have anyone to comfort them at the time or were even shouted at for being sick. Others report a sense of vomiting feeling 'violent' or feeling as if they were losing control over their body. When such feelings are experienced in the body, as well as strong emotions such as fear, it is likely that further episodes of vomiting will lead to extreme anxiety. Other factors then come into play to keep this fear going. We will cover these in more detail later in this chapter.

Can you remember any specific incidents involving vomiting when you were young? If so, and you feel able to, write about it here, specifically including your thoughts and feelings at the time.

· ·

· ·

· ·

· ·

· ·

· ·

· ·

· ·

· ·

· ·

· ·

Some people with emetophobia cannot remember a frightening episode of vomiting in their childhood, and do not know why their phobia developed. In these cases, it is likely that there are other factors involved.

Factors in a person's environment

A person's environment may be important in leading to a fear of vomiting. These can include:

- Having over-protective parents
- Abuse around the time of a frightening early episode of vomiting
- Other distressing experiences such as witnessing a loved one vomit and become seriously ill.

Another important factor in the development of emetophobia is physical illness. For example, experiencing a vomiting bug or food poisoning at a vulnerable time may lead to an extreme fear of vomiting. These factors are beyond the person's control, and it is never their fault that they experience anything like this. It is very understandable that an experience of vomiting when a person is already very distressed would lead them to be very afraid of being sick again.

Write down any factors in your environment that you think might be important.

. . . .

. . . .

. . . .

. . . .

. . . .

Personality and psychological factors

Some people may have certain personality traits, or they may think and feel in certain ways that make them more vulnerable to developing emetophobia. Research has shown that people with emetophobia have a stronger sense of 'internal control'. This means they believe they are able to control whether they vomit or not. However, this is only a belief, as there is no evidence that someone can control whether they vomit or not. Some people with emetophobia may also be more sensitive to the emotions of anxiety and disgust. This may cause them to react more strongly and negatively to early episodes of vomiting. Lastly, some people are more vulnerable to 'somatization'. This is the tendency to express anxiety through physical symptoms such as nausea, bloating, diarrhoea and 'butterflies'. In these cases, emetophobia may be more likely to develop when anxiety is experienced as a physical symptom, such as nausea. This is then understood to be evidence that vomiting is likely, which leads to strong feelings of fear.

Write down any aspects of your personality that might have contributed towards developing emetophobia.

. . . .

. . . .

. . . .

. . . .

. . . .

Biological and genetic factors

Often phobias like emetophobia can have genetic influences. If an individual has an immediate relative with depression or an anxiety disorder, they may be more likely to have difficulties themselves. Phobias can also be learned, for example from seeing a close loved one react negatively to being sick or seeing another person vomit. This may teach an individual that it is something to be afraid of and they may then fear vomiting. It is important to say here that mental health problems can be common. Remember that just because a close relative may have difficulties with anxiety or phobias, it does not mean that you will have them too. It is most likely that phobias develop due to a combination of different reasons. Try not to worry about being more at risk than others.

Write down any biological or genetic influences here.

. . . .

. . . .

. . . .

. . . .

. . . .

What keeps emetophobia going?

In the previous chapter, we looked at the typical features of emetophobia. We described the experiences that may be common among people who have it. In this chapter, we will start to piece these together and explore how these features can keep the problem going. This follows a cognitive behavioural model or understanding of emetophobia.

People with emetophobia tend to believe that thoughts, images or feelings of nausea or feeling bloated mean that they are about to vomit. We think this may be due to a past experience of vomiting when they were young. In emetophobia, vomiting is usually judged as 100 per cent awful and interpreted as meaning they will lose control and fear they cannot prevent themselves from being sick.

There is often an intolerance of uncertainty – that not knowing whether one is going to be sick or not is worse than being sick. This thinking style is then associated with feeling extremely anxious and panicky. These emotional responses happen very quickly as this is how the threat system is designed to work – to initiate a fast response in order to keep us safe from threat. These emotional responses trigger the release of adrenaline, which is likely to lead to increased nausea and physical sensations. This starts a vicious circle in motion, which looks like this:

It does not really matter what comes first as it all happens so quickly and each feeling is fused with another. Once this vicious circle is established it is kept going by several processes. This section will explain how many of these processes make sense. We believe them to be very understandable strategies that are intended to reduce anxiety and avoid vomiting in the short term. However, we will learn how these processes can in fact be very unhelpful over time, and the very reason that your anxiety and the problem itself continues!

Worry, reassurance and mental planning

If you have emetophobia, you may believe that you are about to be sick, and you may try really hard to plan mentally how to stop yourself vomiting. You may think how you can avoid others who might vomit, or how to escape situations. You may spend a lot of time worrying in order to prevent the worst from happening. It's common to reassure yourself and ask for reassurance from others. These processes are understandable and may feel helpful to you in managing your anxiety and reducing the chances of your worst fears happening. However, they actually keep you focused on the problem and increase your doubts. They then make the idea of vomiting seem much more likely and awful if it does in fact happen. Over time, these processes keep your anxiety and emetophobia going.

Self-focused attention and looking for danger

When you worry about vomiting, you may find your attention turning inwards to monitor what your body and your digestive system are doing. This is especially likely if you feel sensations that make you very concerned about vomiting. You might also want to keep an eye out for signs of danger in your immediate environment. You might do this in order to watch out for things around you that may make you or other people more at risk of vomiting. These may feel like sensible things to do in order to monitor the likelihood that you could be about to vomit, as they may help you to stop it.

However, turning your attention inwards and looking for danger can be very unhelpful. They keep vomiting at the forefront of your mind. In the long run, this makes you more anxious about it and makes the prospect of vomiting seem much worse. This also can have the effect of making bodily sensations seem worse or more noticeable, especially if you are anxious. What may be harmless and totally unrelated sensations – or sensations that are in fact caused by anxiety – can often seem much scarier. They can also be seen as a false alarm that you are about to vomit if you are thinking about them or trying to notice them often. Lastly, this self-monitoring can really make you feel as if you can control whether or not you vomit. However, if you do really need to vomit, this is a reflex that is impossible to control. In Chapter 3, we will discuss why this is a good thing for your survival!

Avoidance

When you are afraid of something, it is a very common reaction to want to avoid it. Initially this makes you feel less afraid. In emetophobia, common things that are avoided include:

- Certain types of food or restaurants
- Travel abroad
- Public transport
- Going out to bars or pubs or crowded places
- Ill people
- Children
- Medications or operations.

In the short term, this makes sense to you as it makes you feel as if you are less likely to vomit, which makes you feel less anxious. However, over time, the anxiety around vomiting continues to get worse and worse. This is because you never learn that:

- the risk of something bad actually happening may be far smaller than you think it is
- you can usually cope better than you think you can in many situations.

Through avoidance, you learn that escaping a situation feels good because your anxiety reduces initially. However, the next time you encounter the same feared situation, you are still very anxious, perhaps even more so.

The other problem with avoiding situations and activities is that in trying to reduce your anxiety, you actually become controlled by it. You miss out on what is important to you, such as meeting friends at a particular restaurant, going on holiday to exciting places or being able to feel comfortable in busy environments. It is very common in emetophobia that life becomes restricted because anxiety and fear take away the very things that you value and enjoy doing. What you fail to learn by avoiding these situations is that actually if you continue to face your fears then you may experience the initial anxiety but in time this reduces. Anxiety cannot last forever – that would be exhausting and physically impossible! By doing what you are afraid of, you learn that it may not be as bad as you think. This is how avoidance can make anxiety build over time in emetophobia. You need to be working on the opposite of avoidance: facing your fears. We will discuss this in more detail in Chapters 3 and 5.

Safety-seeking and compulsive behaviours

Safety-seeking behaviours are strategies used to reduce anxiety or the chances of vomiting when escape or avoidance is not possible. Examples include:

- Checking sell-by dates of food
- Frequent hand washing or cleaning
- Eating mints or chewing gum
- Drinking bottled water
- Doing mental activities such as repeating phrases in your head, or avoiding 'the 13th stair'
- Taking anti-nausea medication.

All these strategies are motivated by a desire to feel safe by reducing nausea or the chance of vomiting. This helps you to feel less anxious in certain situations. These strategies are completely understandable given how scared you might feel at the thought of vomiting or being around someone who is vomiting. When we are very afraid, it is only natural to want to protect ourselves from the thing that we feel is a threat to our safety or our health. However, much like the other processes, these strategies can actually be very unhelpful. Safety-seeking behaviours are one of the main reasons the problem persists or gets worse over time. These strategies convince us that we have control over the situation (when maybe we don't or shouldn't have). They confirm the idea in our heads that vomiting is really, really awful and scary and should be avoided at all costs. Safety-seeking behaviours also prevent us from learning what our feared situation is really like (e.g. 'Phew, that was a close one – if I hadn't repeated my lucky phrase then maybe I could have vomited'). As a result, we miss opportunities to learn that maybe it is different or not as bad as our beliefs. This in turn makes us feel a lot more anxious, a lot more focused on the problem and, in the long term, the problem itself just keeps going or getting bigger.

Bringing it all together – the vicious flower model

We have covered the most common processes that keep the problem of emetophobia going. This can be seen in the following diagram that represents a 'vicious flower'. The central part of the 'flower' in emetophobia is the middle circle outlining the physical sensations, thoughts, anxiety and images/pictures. The 'petals' are the processes that keep the central fear in emetophobia going over time and feed the preoccupation and distress. Therapists may refer to this as a 'formulation' or understanding of what keeps the problem going. It is important because you will need to take away the petals that are maintaining the distress of your emetophobia.

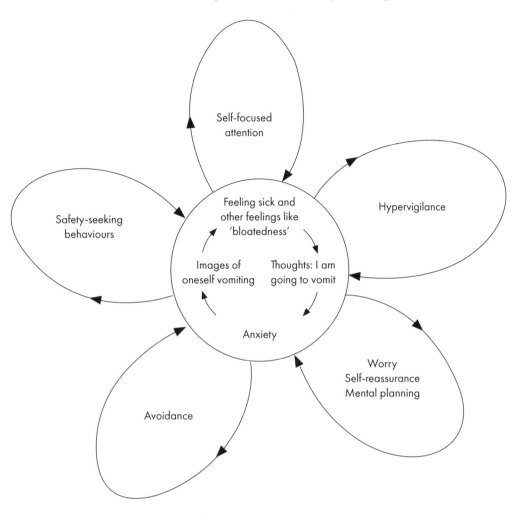

We will now use Sally as an example to illustrate how her emetophobia was maintained.

You will remember that when Sally was eight years old she saw a classmate being sick in a school assembly. She remembers this being very sudden and there was a big commotion. She felt very frightened at the time as she did not know what was going on straight away. She remembers the girl looking very upset, and two teachers rushing forward to help her. Ever since this episode, she has been very afraid that she will be sick herself. She remembered thinking that it must have been awful for the girl and she must have felt very afraid herself at the time. Sally does not recall ever being sick herself until this point. She believes that if she is sick she will not be able to stop it. Sally often feels very nauseous and because of this she worries that she could be sick at any moment and without warning. This causes her to feel very anxious. This makes her feel more nauseous and the vicious circle continues.

In order to manage her nausea and fear, she avoids eating foods she believes to be unsafe, such as chicken or seafood. She does not eat at restaurants or friends' houses if she is unsure how the food has been handled and cooked. She also avoids ill people or children who might vomit. She avoids enclosed spaces, such as travel on public transport. Through avoiding these situations, the risks of vomiting seem huge to Sally. She is never able to learn that in reality the risk of getting food poisoning is relatively small. She also never learns that the chances of seeing ill and/or drunk people who are vomiting are much lower than she thinks.

Sally uses safety-seeking behaviours to stop herself getting ill and vomiting. She always carries an antibacterial gel with her in her handbag wherever she goes. She washes her hands excessively. She takes small sips of water and chews mints to manage her nausea and reduce the likelihood of vomiting unexpectedly. These strategies have the unintended consequence of convincing Sally that vomiting will be really awful and uncontrollable. This makes the problem seem much bigger for her. Sally constantly looks out for signs of danger in her environment, such as someone else vomiting. She monitors her body for evidence of nausea or being unwell. She asks friends and family for reassurance that she will not vomit frequently. These strategies serve to keep Sally very focused on the problem and her symptoms, and she feels much more anxious as a result.

Here is Sally's vicious flower model:

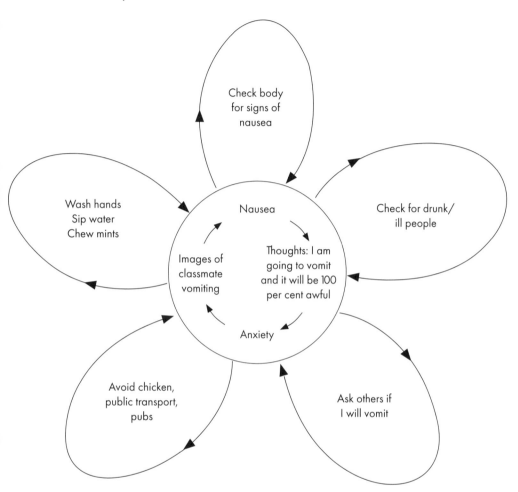

Now it's your turn. Make a list of any processes that you think may be making your anxiety worse and keeping the problem going. Write them down in the vicious flower diagram below. Which of these strategies might be unhelpful to you? It's okay if the processes you identify for yourself are different from the ones we have already mentioned, or you can think of new ones that haven't been discussed. The important thing is that the diagram is about you and your situation, and that it makes sense to you.

Your vicious flower model:

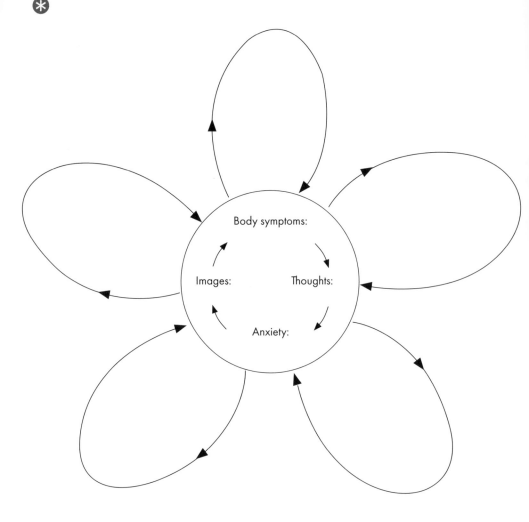

Body symptoms:

Images:

Thoughts:

Anxiety:

Chapter summary

- Emetophobia is caused by many factors, not just one.
- These can include early life experiences, environmental factors, personality or psychological traits, and biological or genetic factors.
- The emotional responses of fear, disgust, anger and shame can play an important role in developing and maintaining emetophobia.
- It is very common for emetophobia to develop after a difficult episode of vomiting that happens at an early age.
- Whatever caused your phobia, it is not your fault that you have it and you are not alone.
- Many of the features of emetophobia seem helpful in reducing your anxiety and the chance of vomiting; however, they are often unhelpful and actually keep the problem going.
- The vicious flower diagram can help you to understand how your problem is maintained and how your solutions have become the problem!

CHAPTER 3

An Introduction to Cognitive Behavioural Therapy for Emetophobia

What is cognitive behavioural therapy?

Cognitive behavioural therapy – or CBT – is a talking and doing therapy that aims to reduce psychological distress by working with people's thoughts and actions. The way we feel about vomiting may be down to the associations that we have made from the past. Let's use an example. Imagine that you started to feel nauseous or have an image of being sick for no reason. You immediately think to yourself, *I must have eaten something dodgy or caught something*, while you feel very panicky and even more sick. You believe you might vomit and lose control, and desperately want to know if you are going to vomit as it is judged as 100 per cent awful and a fate worse than death.

Now let's imagine the same happening to someone who does not fear vomiting. When they start to feel sick, they might wonder what could have caused it. They think, *That's strange, but if I sit quietly for a minute it will probably go away*. In this second example, the same symptom has been understood in a very different way. The thoughts about the situation are neutral, and as a result this person remains calm and does not panic. After a little while, they start to feel better and go about their day.

Now we have seen how thoughts can affect our feelings, can you think how these different thoughts might drive your behaviour? In the first scenario, you were very anxious about feeling sick, and may have spent the rest of the day monitoring your body for signs of illness or worrying about being sick at any time. You might have avoided doing certain things or going to places 'just in case'. This behaviour is likely to have kept your anxiety high throughout the day. In the second example, the person who does not fear vomiting did not engage in any anxious behaviours or avoidance. This might have given them the opportunity to learn that feeling sick is not harmful and does not lead to vomiting. Therefore, they are more likely to feel calmer the next time they feel anything similar; whereas the behaviours in the first scenario may make it hard to break the cycle between your thoughts, feelings and actions. You will continue to fear these symptoms if there is never an opportunity to challenge this way of thinking. In this simple example, we can see how thoughts, feelings, sensations and behaviours all affect each other.

CBT for emetophobia

Research has shown that CBT is an effective treatment for emetophobia. In emetophobia, people usually believe that body sensations are a sign that vomiting is about to happen, that they will lose control and that vomiting will be truly awful. People with emetophobia often want to know for certain that they will not vomit. Such thinking styles are associated with extreme anxiety, safety-seeking behaviours and avoidance. CBT aims to support people to create opportunities to work with these thinking styles and behaviours.

Psycho-education around vomiting

A good place to start in therapy for emetophobia is to learn about why we vomit. Vomiting – even though it can be unpleasant – is actually a really important reflex for humans. We vomit to keep ourselves safe. It is an automatic reflex that we *cannot* control. You may convince yourself that you can control it as it makes you feel less anxious, but there is no evidence that human beings can control an automatic reflex. Vomiting is important for our survival, because it protects us from toxins that we can pick up from our environment. It is actually a really good thing that we cannot control this. If we could decide whether or not we vomited and stop ourselves from vomiting, we would risk being poisoned. Therefore, vomiting is the body's way of ridding itself of harmful poisons that could make us very ill or even die. We know this because of what we know about animals such as rats, horses, rabbits and guinea pigs. These animals are unable to vomit, and this is why rat poison works so well! Rats die from rat poison because their bodies cannot get rid of these toxins by vomiting.

Another thing we know about vomiting is that the body is very clever at controlling this reflex for us until we are better. You cannot control whether you vomit. It might feel as if you can stop yourself from vomiting (because you don't vomit) but there is no known mechanism for stopping yourself from vomiting. If you could, then surely it would be dangerous to not get rid of the toxins. Try not to fight or control the feeling of anxiety about vomiting. This will make your feelings of anxiety last longer.

Even if you do vomit, it will not go on and on for a long time without stopping. Our bodies cannot vomit forever! There is nothing left in the stomach. Even when people have food poisoning or a sickness that lasts a few days, they report short episodes of vomiting that have a clear beginning and end. Nausea and vomiting may last a few minutes, but do not continue forever. Often people report that vomiting actually makes them feel a lot better – possibly because they have got rid of the toxin that was making them ill. So, vomiting in itself is not dangerous, but in fact a very natural and important reflex in helping us to survive and stay well.

Lastly, we know that other people rarely react to vomiting in the way we might expect. In surveys that we have conducted to collect information on reactions to vomiting, most people react with kindness and compassion and feel driven to help. It is far more likely that people will check if you are okay, as it is in our instinct to care for others. It may be that people do not respond in this situation; however, this does not mean that they are judging you or thinking badly of you.

Theory A and Theory B

In CBT for emetophobia there are two ways of thinking about the problem: *Theory A* and *Theory B*. Theory A might be that you are at risk of vomiting at any time; that vomiting is so awful that it is a fate worse than death; that you must therefore know whether you are going to vomit or not; that if you do vomit, you will lose control and it will go on forever. If this is true then you need to be very careful about where you go, what you eat and what you do. You should engage in lots of safety-seeking behaviours and monitor yourself and others. We should do all this to reduce the risk of vomiting. Can you think how Theory A might affect your life and the way you feel? What will your future look like if you are avoiding things you enjoy, and worrying a lot about keeping safe?

If Theory A is true, what do you need to do about it?

. . . .

. . . .

. . . .

. . . .

. . . .

Now let's think about another *less threatening* way to think about the problem: Theory B. Theory B tells us that vomiting is very unpleasant but you can bear it. You cannot be in control of your vomiting, but you can tolerate not knowing whether you are going to vomit. This theory says that it's your anxiety telling you that you must not vomit at all costs. If Theory B is true, what do you need to do? If there is no threat, then safety-seeking behaviours, avoidance and monitoring are no longer needed. You no longer need to worry about what you are doing, who you are seeing and what you are eating, as vomiting is not likely. If Theory B is true, what does your life look like? How do you feel? And what does your future look like if you are free to live your life in the way that you would like to without anxiety calling the shots?

If Theory B is true, what do you need to do about it?

. . . .

. . . .

. . . .

. . . .

. . . .

These theories form the basis of CBT for emetophobia. For the purpose of moving forward towards a life without emetophobia, we assume that Theory B is 100 per cent true (even if you don't believe it). This helps to guide us where we go next in therapy. Theory B tells us that the things we are doing such as avoidance and safety-seeking behaviours are not necessary. People are then supported to stop doing them, and to engage in meaningful activities and a life that is 100 per cent theirs.

Exposure

One of the biggest tools used in CBT to help us to do this is called 'exposure' or facing up to your fears. You will remember in the previous chapter we talked about the role of avoidance. This serves to confirm to people that their scary thoughts are correct, and they can avoid the worst from happening by simply avoiding what is feared. Over time, this keeps anxiety and the fear of vomiting going. However, in CBT we encourage people *to do the opposite*. We want them to approach the very things they are avoiding. This is likely to sound very scary to someone with emetophobia, but it is extremely important! This is for two reasons:

1. It helps you to learn that what you fear is not as accurate or awful as you think it is.
2. It helps to build resilience and the idea that you can cope much better than you expect.

Another very important part of overcoming emetophobia is to encourage you to *stop using your safety-seeking behaviours*. You might have heard this called 'exposure and response prevention' (ERP), whereby people are encouraged to face their feared situations while dropping safety-seeking and compulsive behaviours. You might read this and think this is unhelpful as those strategies help you to cope with your anxiety. However, we know that these strategies are one of the main reasons your anxiety continues. People with emetophobia use these strategies in feared situations they cannot avoid. They believe that these strategies make things better in the short term because they feel less anxious. Therefore, they start to think that vomiting is controllable, and only didn't happen because they washed their hands, or avoided eating at that restaurant. However, what we hope people will learn in CBT is that actually vomiting is a possibility, but if it happens it will be okay and they can cope with it. Safety-seeking behaviours will never allow you to learn this, as they are designed to stop the worst from happening. We will discuss this more in Chapter 5 when we come to outlining these techniques in more detail.

It is important to note here that, in CBT for emetophobia, you will never be asked to do something that is likely to make you vomit. We never make a person with emetophobia vomit on purpose. This is not likely to reduce anxiety and is not thought to be helpful or necessary. You will also never be encouraged to do something that feels so hard or scary that you can't do it. Every aspect of treatment is done with your agreement, and at a time when you feel able to participate. We acknowledge that this process will require you to try things that will challenge you and may feel very anxiety provoking, but it is important to get the level of anxiety right. We need it to be just challenging enough, to give you the opportunity to learn something new, but not so challenging that you stop altogether. For this reason, exposure is usually done in a *graded* way. This means we often start with something small to give confidence and start you on your way to learning. We then build on this learning each time. The idea is to work your way towards engaging in things that are meaningful to you, without anxiety and fear. However, research shows that treatment is more effective if you then jump around the different levels of this hierarchy. You might go from easy targets to more difficult ones and in as many different situations or contexts as possible.

Working with images

Imagery re-scripting

One last element of CBT for some people with emetophobia is called *imagery re-scripting*. We know that it is common for people with emetophobia to remember a difficult early experience of vomiting. In many cases, these early experiences are one of the factors that can lead to emetophobia. Many people experience images and other sensations that relate to these experiences. These can cause anxiety, and keep the problem going. In CBT, we often try to work with early experiences of vomiting that still cause distress. We do this by asking people to describe their early experiences of vomiting with their eyes closed. We ask them to talk through the experience in a lot of detail, and in the first person. People are also asked to use the present tense, as if it is happening again now. Ideally, we want people to revisit this experience, including as many senses and feelings from the time as possible. We then identify what the young person needed at the time: a friendly face, someone to rescue them, someone to be kind and give them a hug? We encourage the person to imagine themselves as an adult providing that care and support. This is done until all these needs are met and the person feels better. We will cover all these aspects of therapy in more detail in Chapter 5. You will have the chance to think how they apply to you, and to work on some specific things for yourself.

Eye Movement Desensitization and Reprocessing (EMDR)

Other practitioners have tried an approach known as EMDR. This aims to replicate a natural function of the body during rapid eye-movement (REM) sleep, which processes emotional responses to trauma. An EMDR therapist will pass their finger back and forth in front of your face and ask you to follow their hand movements with your eyes while you recall a disturbing event. This can help to process the emotions linked with past aversive memories of vomiting. It also helps to decrease the sense of 'nowness' that can be linked to past memories. This approach has not been fully investigated in emetophobia, but may be useful as it overlaps with imagery re-scripting. It must be done with the support of a professional trained in EMDR and should not be done alone without a programme of exposure.

Overcoming emetophobia – examples of CBT in action

Sally

During Sally's treatment, she wanted to engage in situations that she had been avoiding. She felt this would allow her to learn a different way of thinking about her problem. She made a list of situations that would challenge her. She wanted to start with food and addressing her eating habits first. She then wanted to work her way up to spending time with her friend's children and visiting her aunt in hospital. She started by eating very small amounts of chicken and fish. She tried very hard not to wash her hands; to stop sipping water; and to focus on a nice activity instead of her stomach afterwards. She initially found this hard to start, but once she did, she felt very proud of herself. She was surprised to find that although she was anxious, she was not sick. She decided to see if this was just good luck and tested herself again by letting her friend cook her lunch. Again, she tried to be present in the moment. She tried hard not to monitor her body for signs of sickness. She also resisted asking her friend for reassurance about how the food was cooked. This time not only was she not sick again, but she found she really enjoyed her friend's company and the food she cooked!

Sally gradually started to feel less anxious around food, and she found herself gaining some of the weight she lost. Encouraged by these successes, she arranged to meet her friend and her 5-year-old in a local park. She was surprised again to learn that the child was not ill, and she herself did not become sick. This led her to feel able to tackle one of her biggest challenges. She went to visit her aunt in hospital. When she was there, she felt it was very important to resist the urge to wash her hands and ask her aunt if she felt sick. She even bought a sandwich from the shop! Sally learnt again that the risk of getting ill and being sick was very small, even in a hospital environment. Sally started to think that actually her problem was best explained by Theory B; that her worry and behaviours were the problem, and she did not need to be so anxious. She found her confidence growing and she was able to do more and more. She visited friends for meals at their houses, went to the pub and was able to travel by public transport. Sally felt that she was starting to live her life in a meaningful way again, as she was in control of what she did and not the phobia. She felt really proud of herself that she had come so far.

Jon

Jon felt as if he had had emetophobia for most of his life and it was time to make some changes. He felt sad that he had missed out on so many things he enjoyed. He felt very motivated to overcome his fears of getting ill and vomiting. Treatment started with supporting Jon to learn about the functions of vomiting, and why it is helpful. He was also supported to learn a more realistic view of what vomiting is like, to help adjust his expectations that it would be violent and long lasting. He started to develop a more rational understanding that vomiting occurs in short episodes, and despite it being unpleasant, he and his body could cope with it. This information already helped Jon to feel less anxious in relation to vomiting. This enabled Jon to start to test out Theory B! He was able to start visiting public places like shops and restaurants, and to use public transport. Eventually, he went to a hospital and was able to see that it was not as bad as he imagined and was surprised to see that this did not make him at all ill!

Once he felt more confident, he visited a friend who had recently been ill. He found this to be a really nice experience, and started to socialize more, which lifted his mood. Jon was supported to stop looking for trouble by researching outbreaks of illnesses and symptoms to watch out for on the internet. This helped to reduce his preoccupation with viruses and getting ill. Jon's biggest goal was to go on holiday with his friend. Eventually, he was able to book a weekend away and felt very proud that he managed to achieve this. He also learned that he was able to do things he enjoyed without getting sick, and that maybe the risks of getting ill were smaller than he thought. Lastly, Jon was supported to think about his early experiences of vomiting and the difficult emotions he experienced at the time. He identified that he really needed to be cared for and shown kindness and compassion at the time, instead of anger. He was able to imagine this for himself, which made him feel that being sick is just something that happens instead of something to be ashamed about. This really helped Jon to be more accepting of vomiting and less afraid.

Now have a think about which parts of CBT for emetophobia might be most helpful for you. What might you like to try out?

. . . .

. . . .

. . . .

. . . .

. . . .

. . . .

. . . .

Pros and cons of change

We understand that, at this point, it can be difficult to contemplate the prospect of change. It is very normal to feel daunted by the techniques we have introduced. If you are finding it difficult to think about starting to change your behaviours, then it can be helpful to consider what might be helpful and unhelpful about making such changes. We call this *the pros and cons of change*. Fill in the spaces below to help you.

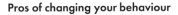

Pros of changing your behaviour	Cons of changing your behaviour

Now take a look at both columns and weigh them up. Is one side longer than the other? How might you benefit from committing to doing this behaviour less? How might this help you to achieve your goals? How has this exercise helped you in deciding whether this behaviour is a helpful process in your life?

Sally's pros and cons of change

Sally was preparing to make some changes to her thinking styles and behaviours in order to overcome her emetophobia. However, this made her feel anxious because she had experienced emetophobia for so long, it was difficult to imagine her life without it. Her safety-seeking behaviours and perceived certainty that she would not vomit made her feel safe, and she was daunted by the prospect of doing things differently. She decided to consider the pros and cons of change. This helped her to see that the benefits far outweighed the negatives, and she was able to envisage a far brighter future without emetophobia. This gave her the motivation and courage to make a start.

Pros of changing your behaviour	Cons of changing your behaviour
I will be able to enjoy food again and go to more restaurants/try different foods.	I will feel very anxious.
I will be able to nourish my body so that I am strong and healthy.	I will have to give up the 'certainty' that gives me a sense of comfort.
I will be able to be more present in the moment and enjoy valued activities instead of worrying about vomiting all the time.	I will have to accept that I might one day vomit in order to have the life I want.
My relationships will be better as I can focus my energy on being with other people without worry or seeking reassurance – people will enjoy my company more.	
I will be able to spend time with my friends with kids, and visit my aunt when she is sick.	
I will be able to have children and a family of my own.	

Other psychological treatments for emetophobia

The current evidence base for treatment of emetophobia is limited. CBT, including exposure, is the only treatment approach to be investigated by a randomized controlled trial (RCT), which is the gold standard in researching effective treatments. When a group is randomized to different treatment, it tells us whether on average one treatment is better than another credible alternative treatment. Other forms of therapy such as psychotherapy, rational therapies and trauma-focused approaches such as EMDR and hypnotherapy are yet to be investigated by RCT or compared against CBT. Therefore, there is no scientific evidence to suggest that these approaches have any benefit in treating emetophobia. There is a need for further research by RCT comparing CBT and other approaches against a credible alternative to determine if other treatments have any benefit. If you are receiving any type of psychological treatment from a trained professional, then it's important to ask about what protocol they are following, and the evidence base for the model they are using to help you.

Chapter summary

- CBT works on the principle that the way we feel about a situation depends on what we think about it.
- In emetophobia, people feel anxious about vomiting because they think it will be awful and they will be out of control.
- Treatment focuses on two theories or ways of thinking about the problem: Theory A (a threat problem) and Theory B (a worry problem).
- Theory B tells us that the problem is not vomiting itself, but the things we do to manage our anxiety and stop ourselves from vomiting – and this is what we need to change to feel better.
- CBT for emetophobia encourages people to face their fears and be 'exposed' to situations that make them feel anxious – this helps them to learn what these situations are really like, not what anxiety tells them they will be like.
- CBT also encourages people to stop using safety-seeking behaviours that make anxiety worse.
- In some cases, people may be supported to work with their distressing memories of vomiting and any images or pictures that cause them to feel anxious.
- Be sceptical of any practitioner who claims they can 'cure' your emetophobia by using an easy or simple approach. It will take a lot of courage on your part to face your fears.

CHAPTER 4

———

Defining your Problems and Goals

This chapter will help you to define your emetophobia – to understand how serious it is, and how much it affects your day-to-day life. It is helpful to do this before you begin any treatment so that you have a starting point to compare your progress later. This will give you a sense of how much change there has been in your symptoms over time. There are two scales that are used to define your current difficulties, and how much they impact on your life: the Specific Phobia of Vomiting Inventory (SPOVI) and the Emetophobia Questionnaire (EmetQ).

Measuring your symptoms

The Specific Phobia of Vomiting Inventory (SPOVI)[1]

Each statement in the SPOVI consists of five possible responses and each response scores a number of points. Tick the box that best describes how your fear of vomiting has affected you *over the past week*. The options are as follows: not at all (0 points), a little (1 point), often (2 points), a lot (3 points) and all the time (4 points). Once you have answered each question, you can get a total score by adding up the points for every question. The more points you have, the more severe your emetophobia is likely to be. You are likely to have emetophobia if you score 10 or more. On average, people with emetophobia score about 30. Remember that the questionnaire is just a helpful way to see how your symptoms change over time. Successful treatment might reasonably expect scores on the SPOVI during treatment to reduce by roughly 20 points over time, if things are going well. However, a reduction of 11 points or more would be regarded as a reliable improvement.

1   Veale, D., Ellison, N., Boschen, M., Costa, A. *et al.* (2013). 'Development of an inventory to measure Specific Phobia of Vomiting (emetophobia).' *Cognitive Therapy and Research*, 37, 595–604. https://dx.doi.org/10.1007/s10608-012-9495-y.

	Not at all (0)	A little (1)	Often (2)	A lot (3)	All the time (4)
1. I have been worrying about myself or others vomiting.					
2. I have been avoiding adults or children because of my fear of vomiting.					
3. I have been avoiding situations or activities because of my fear of vomiting.					
4. I have been trying to find reasons to explain why I feel nauseous.					
5. I have been avoiding objects that other people have touched because of my fear of vomiting.					
6. I have been focused on whether I feel ill and could vomit rather than on my surroundings.					
7. I have been looking at others to see if they may be ill and vomiting.					
8. If I think I am going to vomit, I do something to try to stop myself from vomiting.					
9. I have been trying to avoid or control any thoughts or images about vomiting.					
10. I have been restricting the amount or type of food I eat or alcohol I drink because of my fear of vomiting.					
11. I have been feeling nauseous.					
12. I have been thinking about how to stop myself or others from vomiting.					

13. I have been seeking reassurance that I
or others will not be ill and vomit.

14. I have escaped from situations
because I am afraid I or others may
vomit.

TOTAL

The Emetophobia Questionnaire – 13 (EmetQ-13)[2]

The EmetQ-13 measures behaviours and beliefs that are very common in emetophobia. There are 13 items, and answers range from 1 (strongly disagree) to 5 (strongly agree). Rate how much you agree with each of the statements *over the last week*, indicating your response by circling the appropriate number next to each question. Try to answer as many questions as you can without using the 'unsure' response, then add up your scores using the numbers provided. A higher total score is likely to mean that your emetophobia makes you very anxious and has a bigger impact on your day-to-day life. You are likely to have emetophobia if you score more than 22.

On average, people with emetophobia score about 38. A good outcome on the EmetQ would be a reduction in a score of roughly 14 points.

2   Boschen, M., Veale, D., Ellison, N. and Reddell, T. (2013). 'The Emetophobia Questionnaire (EmetQ-13): psychometric validation of a measure of specific phobia of vomiting.' *Journal of Anxiety Disorders*, 27(7), 670–677. https://dx.doi.org/10.1016/j.janxdis.2013.08.004.

1	2	3	4	5
Strongly disagree	Disagree	Unsure	Agree	Strongly agree

1. Exposure to vomit can cause sickness and/or illness.	1	2	3	4	5
2. If I see vomit, I may be sick myself.	1	2	3	4	5
3. If I smell vomit I may be sick myself.	1	2	3	4	5
4. I notice physical anxiety symptoms when exposed to vomit.	1	2	3	4	5
5. I avoid places where others may vomit.	1	2	3	4	5
6. I avoid adults who may be likely to vomit.	1	2	3	4	5
7. I avoid children who may be likely to vomit.	1	2	3	4	5
8. I avoid fast-moving activities like rides at the theme park, because I may vomit.	1	2	3	4	5
9. I avoid sea travel (boats, etc.) because I may become nauseous or vomit.	1	2	3	4	5
10. I avoid air travel because I may become nauseous or vomit.	1	2	3	4	5
11. I avoid other forms of transport because I may become nauseous or vomit.	1	2	3	4	5
12. I avoid places where there is no medical attention, because I may become nauseous or vomit.	1	2	3	4	5
13. I avoid places where there are no facilities to cater if I become nauseous or vomit.	1	2	3	4	5

TOTAL

Once you have added up your total scores, make a note of them in the worksheet below. Use the top row to record the week number or date.

Measure	
SPOVI	
EmetQ	

Remember to complete both questionnaires every week or fortnight to record your progress over time. You might notice that your scores on the SPOVI change more quickly than those on the EmetQ. This is common, as the two questionnaires measure slightly different things and the SPOVI is slightly more sensitive to change. If your scores seem high at the start, try not to worry. It is not your fault for getting a high score, and it does not mean that the treatment will not work. These treatments have been shown to help people who show severe symptoms of emetophobia, so there is every reason to hope that you can begin to tackle your anxiety no matter what your scores are at the start. The important part is that you *begin to see them changing*, not what scores you start off with.

Defining your valued directions

Before you start to make any changes to your thoughts and behaviour, it is important to understand what you are working towards. At the start of treatment, it is helpful to think about what is important to you and the things that you value as a person. It is also important to think about specific areas in your life where emetophobia is making it hard to live in line with your values. This helps to focus the changes you make and sets out exactly what treatment might look like for you.

As we have seen in previous chapters, emetophobia can affect many areas of your life. This can include what you eat and drink, your relationships with family, partners and friends, your work or education, travel and leisure activities. It is very common for some of these areas to be more affected than others, or for all of them to be equally affected.

Take some time to think about what is important to you in relation to each of the domains set out in the worksheet below. Describe your values in detail for each domain, and rate how important it is for you out of 10. Finally, think about how your anxiety is affecting how well you are living in line with your values for each area in your life. These values are based on the most common ones for adults, but if you feel that some are not relevant to you right now, then skip to the next one.

Domain	Description of your values	Importance (out of 10)	How emetophobia impacts this value
Family			
Relationships/intimacy			
Parenting			
Friendships/social life			
Career/employment			
Education/personal development			
Fun/leisure			
Spirituality			
Citizenship/environment/community			
Health/physical well-being			

Setting SMART goals

It is helpful to think about the areas in your life that are most affected by your emetophobia, as this helps you to know what you need to change. We do this by setting goals. Working towards goals is easiest when these goals are 'SMART':

Specific. Try to define the goal as much as possible, in as much detail and using very clear language. It is most helpful to have very clear goals, instead of vague ideas; for example, 'To be able to eat chicken without overcooking it or checking the sell-by date before I cook it' *instead of* 'To improve my eating.'

Measurable. It is often helpful if you can measure the progress of a goal, and its outcome. For example, you might define the number of times you want to achieve something, or how much of an activity you want to achieve. This helps us to know that your goal has been achieved. Using a percentage or a number out of 10 can often help here to monitor progress over time; for example, 'To use the Tube to go to work three times per week' or 'To reduce my hand washing by 50 per cent.'

Attainable. You want to be setting realistic goals that are achievable given your current situation. There is no point setting a goal that is very difficult or not attainable, otherwise this is setting you up to fail and you might be tempted to stop working towards it altogether. Therefore, it is important to make these goals just enough to push you out of your comfort zone, but not so difficult that you can't ever get there.

Relevant. Try to focus on goals that are important to you and fall in line with your values as a person. Will the goal meet your needs, and does it fit with your longer-term plans?

Timely. All goals should have a time limit. A short-term goal might be achieved over the next month, a medium-term goal might be for the next six months, and long-term goals may include targets for the next year or two. It is important to set a time limit, as this helps you to know which goals to prioritize and when, and keeps you motivated to work towards them.

On the following page there is a way for you to record your goals at the start of treatment. There is space to enter up to three SMART goals for the short, medium and long term. Use the worksheet to monitor your progress over time.

Time frame	Define the goal	How much/ how often	Monitor outcome	Monitor outcome	Monitor outcome
Short term	1.				
	2.				
	3.				
Medium term	1.				
	2.				
	3.				
Long term	1.				
	2.				
	3.				

How Anna defined her problems and goals

You will remember that Anna developed emetophobia at university after being ill with food poisoning. To cope with her fears of being sick, she restricted what she and her young son ate and spent a lot of time cleaning at home, especially in the kitchen. She avoided seeing family and friends and stopped her son from playing with other children in case he became sick. She and her husband really wanted another child. However, she was too fearful of another pregnancy, and having another small child that could cause her to become unwell. Lastly, she relied on 'mental rituals' such as repeating certain words in her head to keep herself and her family safe.

With her husband's support, Anna decided it was time to overcome her fear of vomiting once and for all. She knew that it was having an impact on many areas of her life, and she really wanted a larger family. Anna thought about what her values were, and the areas of her life that were being impacted by her anxiety.

Domain	Description of your values	Importance (out of 10)	How emetophobia impacts this value
Family/parenting	I really want to have a big family of my own seeing as I have three older brothers. I value family relationships being close and supportive.	10	My fear is stopping me from having more children and is impacting my relationship with my son as I am anxious around him.
Relationships/intimacy	I want to be a caring and attentive partner to my husband.	10	My worries and fears stop me from being present, and limits what we can do as a couple, e.g. eating out.
Friendships/social life	It is important to me to show my friends that I care, and to spend quality time together.	10	My anxiety stops me from seeing my friends and I am spending too much time at home alone.
Career/employment	I value my job and want to be successful and financially independent.	7	My fear makes it hard to focus on work, and I often miss opportunities to travel due to fear of getting ill.
Health/physical well-being	My health is important to me, including my weight and fitness. I also want to enjoy my food.	8	I do not have a healthy and varied diet and I am currently underweight.

Anna felt very sad to see how much her fear was making it difficult to live her life in the ways that were important to her. She felt as if she was getting further and further away from what she wanted. She decided to make a list of goals that felt important to her, and broke these down into short-, medium- and long-term goals.

Time frame	Define the goal	How much/ how often	Monitor outcome	Monitor outcome	Monitor outcome
Short term	1. To eat one 'feared' food every day without cleaning excessively.	Once a day.			
	2. To go to the park with my son for 30 minutes.	Twice a week.			
	3. To go for a meal at a restaurant of their choice with my husband and friends.	Once a week.			
Medium term	1. To go on a work trip abroad with colleagues.	Once every three months.			
	2. To engage in activities I enjoy instead of cleaning.	For 30 minutes, three times a week.			
	3. To stop using mental rituals completely so I can be more present with my loved ones.	100%.			
Long term	1. To weigh myself once per month, and to gain 5kg in weight.	Within the next year.			
	2. To start to try for another baby.	Within the next year.			

Anna decided to monitor her progress every week, and to re-rate her goals in the table above every month for the next year. Short-term and medium-term goals can therefore change every week depending on the progress you make.

Now see if you can do the same and use the table to help you to plan your next steps.

Chapter summary

- It is helpful to use measures to monitor change and progress over time.
- Two questionnaires – the Specific Phobia of Vomiting Inventory and the Emetophobia Questionnaire – can help to identify how severe your emetophobia is.
- Don't worry too much about the numbers at the start, as you are looking for a reduction in scores over time.
- Before you start to make any changes, it can be helpful to think about what is important to you in your life and how emetophobia might be getting in the way.
- You can use this to help you to plan SMART goals that will give you a sense of direction and keep you focused on making changes to the areas of your life that are most important to you.

———

CHAPTER 5

Actively Defeating your Emetophobia

In Chapter 3, we introduced the main features of CBT for emetophobia. In this chapter, we will go into more detail about specific approaches you can use to overcome your difficulties. We recommend that you use the principles of CBT outlined in Chapter 3 to arrive at a good understanding of your emetophobia. This will help you prepare to tackle it head on, rather than just learning to live with it. You will remember that in Chapter 2 we looked at the 'vicious flower' model, which represents the processes that are keeping your emetophobia going. Take a moment now to have a good look at your own version of the model, to remind yourself of the main processes that are relevant for you. This model is the basis for the work we are now going to outline. We will refer to our characters throughout this chapter, to give you real-life examples of CBT techniques in action. If you want to share these with a loved one or someone you are close to, this can be a good way to get some support.

The main principle of CBT for emetophobia is *exposure*. Some therapists will refer to this as behavioural experiments or testing out Theory B, which has a different nuance, but in practice it is much the same in emetophobia.

We will outline how to overcome your emetophobia by confronting your fears *and* testing your predictions as opposed to avoiding or using safety-seeking behaviours. This requires repeated and deliberate practice in order to lessen the impact of your fear and thoughts, and to start living your life in the way you want to and in line with your values – not in the way your emetophobia tells you!

You will remember in Chapter 3 we introduced the idea of two ways of looking at the problem: Theory A and Theory B. We hope that you will have been able to start to develop a more helpful alternative explanation for your thoughts, images and behaviours (Theory B). If you have been living with emetophobia for a long time, then it is likely that you will have accidentally been going along with Theory A and you will have developed many habits that maintain your emetophobia. Using safety-seeking behaviours, seeking reassurance, avoiding feared activities and attending to threat may all be second nature by now. Therefore, learning to challenge these unhelpful ways of coping may require patience, and regular practice. We know that this work is often very difficult, but in our experience the effort is very much worth it for the results. You may find that the longer you have lived with emetophobia, the more effort it takes initially to start to challenge your ways of coping. However, the more effort you put in at the beginning, the more the momentum starts to build, and things will gradually start moving forward.

We recommend that you now start living your life 'as if' Theory B is 100 per cent correct and seeing what happens even if you don't believe it. Over time, you should discover that your emetophobia begins to improve as you learn to tolerate the anxiety rather than avoid vomiting. This will involve doing the exact opposite of what the emetophobia is telling you to do. For example, where it tells you to avoid something, you will approach it head on; where you feel you must use a safety-seeking behaviour, instead you will do more exposure without one. Over the years, it is likely that you have acted to avoid vomiting at all costs, as if it were a fate worse than death. However, the key to overcoming your emetophobia is *accepting the possibility of vomiting and living your life as you want to anyway*. Learning to tolerate not knowing whether you are going to vomit and to spring back if you do vomit is crucial to overcoming this problem. We will briefly outline these techniques first, and then discuss how to carry them out in more detail. It is important to finish reading the whole chapter before you attempt to put the techniques into practice.

Techniques to help to tolerate anxiety

The aim of treatment for emetophobia is to help you to learn to tolerate the uncertainty and the feelings of anxiety and disgust associated with vomiting. To this end, people are often motivated to learn 'techniques' to cope with or reduce their anxiety. However, we suggest that to overcome your emetophobia, it is essential to allow yourself to turn towards your thoughts, feelings and body sensations *without trying to avoid, control or suppress them*. This will involve a great deal of courage to let yourself feel fear while committing to a different response, or rather no response at all! However, we acknowledge that for some people this is very tough and therefore we have included some ideas to help with anxiety before we outline the main elements of therapy.

Slow down your breathing

When you feel anxious, there is often a tendency to breathe fast, which leads to shallow breathing. One effective way to calm yourself down is to purposefully slow down your rate of breathing. This will stimulate your parasympathetic nerve, which slows down your body's physical response to adrenaline. The trick here is to count your in-breaths, and make sure your out-breath is longer by two beats than the in-breath. An example might be that you breathe in for five counts, hold for two and then breathe out for seven counts. It is important that you find the number of counts that work for you, as everyone's breathing is different. Make sure you breathe in right down to your belly, as opposed to just filling your chest, as this will encourage you to breathe deeply, which will slow your breathing. Try to practise these breathing techniques when you feel calm until they become second nature. It will be harder to master these in situations when you are anxious without practising them first.

Reach out to others

When you are very anxious, you may become more self-focused. Try to keep your attention focused externally and reach out to friends and family. Establishing a support network is really important when learning to tolerate anxiety. This may be in person, or over the phone, text or remotely on video. Speaking regularly to others close to you whom you trust can help you to share how you feel and to seek emotional support. Remember that this is different from reassurance seeking. Emotional support from others is different from them providing reassurance that you will not be sick. A hug, sharing a cup of tea, looking at a photo of a loved one or an encouraging text message can go a long way in giving you the courage you need to face your fears.

Cold water

This technique involves briefly submerging your face in very cold water or using an ice pack and light cloth on your forehead. This helps to stimulate your parasympathetic nerve, which is the opposite system to the one that results in physical symptoms of anxiety. This results in slowing your heart rate and relaxing your body. The physical effects are similar to jumping into a very cold pool. It can help to ground you to the here and now if you are feeling very anxious. Other approaches that some people find helpful are sensory oils and toys, and hugging yourself.

Exposure and behavioural experiments

Exposure therapy encourages a person to face their feared situations in a purposeful way. It involves planning to repeatedly and deliberately face your fears *and* to drop your safety-seeking behaviours as you do. You must commit to exposure tasks that will raise your anxiety high enough, and then stay with it for long enough to learn to tolerate the anxiety and uncertainty and test out your predictions of what will happen. A *behavioural experiment* enables you to test out your predictions, for example whether your experience best fits with Theory B. We will refer to these techniques simply as 'exposure' for short, but both exposure and behavioural experiments are a means to the same end. Exposure helps you to learn to tolerate the feelings of anxiety, and experiments allow you to test your expectations of the way your problem works – your anxiety will go on forever and you will lose control (Theory A), or you believe this will happen and everything you are doing to prevent it is actually making things worse (Theory B).

In emetophobia, it is important to plan your exposure tasks no matter how you feel. For exposure to be successful, we want you to feel anxious and nauseous so that you can learn to develop a different way of relating to these experiences. Learning to tolerate something uncomfortable will allow you to get used to it so that your reactions get less and less over time. By acting as if Theory B is 100 per cent true, you will learn that you can tolerate your anxiety and bodily sensations only if you commit to dropping behaviours that maintain emetophobia. Exposure can involve both internal cues such as nausea, and also external situations such as eating foods that are believed to be unsafe or watching a video of someone vomiting.

You might wonder where you would even begin, as the prospect of exposure may seem very daunting. You can use your goals and valued directions to help you to identify the types of situations to include. No matter where you begin it is important to be willing to experience feelings of anxiety, nausea and disgust. It is important to say here that we do not intend for you to feel constantly crippled by such intense anxiety that you cannot move forward. However, it is important that you develop the courage to approach uncomfortable images, thoughts and feelings. It is very normal in these situations to feel anxious, but you must find the courage to begin to tolerate this in order to move forward.

Graded exposure

Exposure is often approached in a graded way using a hierarchy of increasingly difficult situations. This is known as 'graded exposure'. We know that starting to face your fears might seem hugely overwhelming. Therefore, the principle is to start somewhere manageable and 'just challenging enough' before working your way up to more difficult situations. This might help to increase your chances of actually starting instead of avoiding it. Then as you face one small fear and learn from it, you will gain a sense of mastery and confidence in taking on the next challenge. However, we do not want to give the impression that too much anxiety is dangerous and to avoid this you must start exposure slowly. Anxiety in itself may be unpleasant but it cannot harm you. Recent research[1] shows that moving up and down the hierarchy to confront different situations at random is more effective than sticking to a precise order of increasingly difficult situations. This approach has many benefits:

- It will challenge ideas that anxiety should be avoided as it is too uncomfortable – this is not true.
- Higher levels of anxiety will help you to learn to tolerate it quicker.
- It reinforces the idea that to overcome your emetophobia you need to do the opposite of what anxiety tells you.
- It will help you to learn that anxiety and disgust are your body's way of preparing you for a challenge – they are very natural reactions and not a sign that anything bad will happen.

With any exposure tasks, remember it is very important to stay with the anxiety. If you stop during the exposure or go back to avoiding, then you will reinforce the idea that anxiety is harmful. Your anxiety will remain the same and may get even worse. If your

---

1   Craske, M.G., Treanor, M., Conway, C.C., Zbozinek, T. and Vervliet, B. (2014). 'Maximizing exposure therapy: an inhibitory learning approach.' *Behaviour Research and Therapy*, 58, 10–23. https://doi.org/10.1016/j.brat.2014.04.006.

anxiety is lasting for longer than two hours, then you may be using a safety-seeking behaviour or subtly avoiding full exposure without realizing it. If it is too difficult to get on with these exposure tasks, you might need to seek professional help to move forward.

Make a plan for exposure

1. Make an exposure hierarchy

Write down a list of tasks that make up your exposure hierarchy – these are the things you tend to fear or avoid due to your emetophobia and what's important in your life. The list might include situations, activities, places, people and food, as well as vomit-related cues or body sensations. Decide when you will do the task, where you will carry it out, what you might need to help you and how you can do it again in different contexts. Try to put your tasks in order of how much distress they would cause you. To help you, you can use a rating scale of Subjective Units of Distress (SUDs). On this scale, 0 means no distress at all, and 100 is overwhelming distress.

We have included a table below to help you. In the left column, write down each task, and then in the right column record your SUDs rating of how much distress each one would cause you if you did not use safety-seeking behaviours or avoidance. This will help you to list your situations in the right order. So, a situation with a lower anxiety rating would go towards the bottom of the table, and situations closer to 100 would go nearer the top of the table. Remember that this is just to help you to get a list of exposure tasks, and that it is important to move up and down the hierarchy instead of sticking to a precise order of increasingly difficult situations.

Use the worksheet to make your exposure hierarchy. You can use this worksheet to come back to Theory B, to test out whether the results of the tasks best fit this explanation.

✳

Planned exposure task	SUDs rating (0–100)

It is important to note here that we would not recommend that you intentionally make yourself vomit for the purpose of exposure. In our experience, this is rarely helpful or practical. You can use other cues and combinations of cues such as sounds, smells and fake vomit, as well as role play with yourself and others, that work just as well.

Exposure can be to anything related to vomiting that causes anxiety or that you typically avoid. We have created a list of possible situations below. There may be many more that we have not mentioned and that may be useful for you.

Food and eating
- Eating foods that are thought of as unsafe such as poultry, seafood, dairy or foreign meals.
- Eating pre-prepared foods or foods that you have not cooked.
- Eating a larger amount of food than you would typically be used to.
- Eating in a restaurant whose hygiene rating you are unsure of.
- Eating at a time you are not used to.
- Drinking a large amount of fizzy drink quickly.
- Drinking alcohol.

People
- Being close to children.
- Visiting people known to have or have had an illness that causes nausea or vomiting.
- Being close to drunk people.
- Being close to pregnant women.

Places
- Being in busy, over-crowded places or queues.
- Taking public transport.
- Travelling to foreign places.
- Visiting hospitals/A&E departments/GP surgeries.
- Visiting schools/playgrounds.
- Using public toilets.

Experiences
- Going to pubs.
- Travelling by air or sea.
- Going on fairground rides or rollercoasters.

- Taking medications that are known to cause side effects including nausea or sickness.
- Reading in a moving vehicle.

Vomit-related cues

- Putting up pictures of vomiting and posters with the word vomit/sick, or the letter 'V' or 'S', on the walls of your bedroom.
- Repeating out loud the phrase 'I am going to vomit' thousands of times.
- Reading articles about vomiting, nausea or the norovirus (so long as you are not already reading such articles as a way of checking on how to prevent yourself from vomiting).
- Playing with fake vomit and textures of vomit.
- Allowing yourself to experience the smell of vomit, which can be purchased over the internet. The best smell is from butyric acid, but it is difficult to obtain.
- Listening to audio recordings of the sound of retching or vomiting that you can play on a loop. You can find these online by searching on vomit sounds. (It is even more effective if you use smells and fake vomit at the same time!)
- Role-playing – going through the motions of vomiting in a toilet bowl or have someone pretend to vomit in front of you. This is an excellent way of fully accepting that you will probably vomit one day, and it is best to prepare yourself in much the same way as you would for an interview, doing a role play with someone asking relevant questions. There are lots of recipes on the internet for fake vomit that your therapist may use in the toilet bowl, for example cottage cheese, tomato soup, apple juice, tomato juice, soy sauce and frozen mixed vegetables.
- Watching videos, TV shows or movies involving vomit, vomiting, nausea or illness. We recognize that these may not be

that realistic and the sounds and smells of vomiting are usually more powerful stimuli. In the future, we hope to use virtual reality of vomiting as this may be much more realistic than watching others vomit.

- Using a tongue depressor in your mouth to experience gently the sensation of gagging. This will not induce vomiting.

Exposure in imagination
- Imagining a past experience of vomiting.

2. Face your fear

Once you have written down an exposure hierarchy, the next step is to actually get started. The most important thing is to not feel you have to start at the bottom and work your way up in a precise order. It is okay – and preferable! – to jump around the hierarchy, learning to tolerate different situations and gradually building up your sense of resilience. The following points may help you:

- Set a time frame for completing tasks and stick to it.
- Set about facing your fear in a deliberate way for each of the tasks.
- If you find the easier tasks are not challenging enough, try some harder ones – get a friend to help you think of harder ones if needed.
- Have the courage to do the exact things that your emetophobia is telling you not to do – this will not be easy, but it will be worth it in the long run.
- Do the exposure in your imagination first to get you started if you wish, but it is always most effective to do things for real afterwards.

3. Ensure that exposure is for long enough

It is important to ensure that each exposure task is challenging enough and done for long enough. You must face your fear for long enough so that you can learn to tolerate the anxiety, feelings of nausea or disgust. You might find that an exposure task such as eating a new food may make you feel extremely anxious and you rate it very highly on the SUDs scale. This is very understandable given that you are doing the opposite of what you have done for a long time. You are learning to tolerate the anxiety and test your prediction that your experience fits best with Theory B. The longer you stick with each task, the more likely you are to learn that you can tolerate it and that your worst fears did not come true.

Exposure will be even more effective if you can face different scenarios all at once; for example, eating new foods, then getting in a car while imagining being sick. You might find that you need to start with just one of these, which is understandable, but the more situations you can face in one go, the more effective exposure will be. It is not necessary to wait for the anxiety to reduce for each of these exposure tasks, as it may not do so. It is more important that you learn to tolerate the anxiety. You will find that your level of anxiety will reduce each time you repeat the exposure task.

4. Ensure that exposure is frequent enough

Exposure is most effective if it is repeated as often as possible and across different situations. We recommend engaging in exposure tasks at least once every day until you find the anxiety starts to get less in similar situations. If you do not practise every day, then it is likely that your fears will return or get worse the next time you try. If you can manage several exposure tasks per day across different situations, then this will be the most effective way to overcome your emetophobia. It is not possible to do too much exposure! We do not expect that you will notice a reduction in your anxiety during the exposure task. The key is that your anxiety starts to get less the next time you engage in the same task or situation. It is helpful to plan how you can include exposure in your day-to-day life so that you can aim for several times every day.

5. Drop your safety-seeking behaviours

For exposure to be successful, it is crucial to commit to doing the tasks without using any of your safety-seeking behaviours, avoidance, self-focused attention, checking or reassurance-seeking strategies. Remember, it is important to act as if Theory B is 100 per cent true and that these strategies are not necessary as the problem is your fear of vomiting, as opposed to vomiting itself.

The best exposure is going to involve you engaging with the task fully. This will involve being aware of any subtle avoidance that might be going on, for example only eating a very small number of new foods or keeping a small distance away from a sick person as opposed to fully engaging with them. It is also important to be mindful of any safety-seeking behaviours such as reducing the risk of vomiting by taking small sips of water, or mentally reassuring yourself that you will be okay during the exposure task, checking on the internet for signs of norovirus, checking whether you feel ill or checking that others do not look ill. Make sure you have a full list of these safety behaviours and the context in which you use them as they all have to go! Ensuring that you fully drop these strategies will require a great deal of courage, and we know that it is not easy. It may help to be kind to yourself and encourage yourself in a compassionate tone. We discuss this in more detail below. Try to be aware of the emotions you are feeling in each situation and remember that the goal is to learn to tolerate uncomfortable feelings and sensations without trying to avoid, control or blame yourself for experiencing them.

If you are unsure whether you are using safety-seeking behaviours to cope in exposure tasks, then it is helpful to ask yourself what the intention of the behaviour is. A safety-seeking behaviour is anything you are doing that is intended to prevent nausea or vomiting, or to reduce your anxiety or uncertainty about whether you are going to vomit or not. In the long run, these behaviours will serve to strengthen your beliefs about your ability to control or prevent vomiting, the way you rate vomiting as 100 per cent awful and your intolerance of uncertainty. Try to increase your awareness of when and how frequently you engage in these behaviours. When you notice that you are doing them, commit to engaging fully in the task at hand. If what you are doing is truly intended to help you with the exposure as a means to an end so that you repeat it again or do something more anxiety provoking, then it is likely to be a helpful behaviour and you do not need to drop it.

6. Keep a record of your exposure tasks

Keeping a record of your exposure tasks will help you to monitor your progress, and your ability to respond to your fears in a more helpful way. You will be able to keep track of how well you are learning to tolerate uncertainty and uncomfortable feelings and sensations. You can also make notes about any subtle strategies you are using that you might need to work on. On the following page is a worksheet for you to record your exposure tasks.

Exposure task	When/where	What did you learn?	Did you notice any subtle coping strategies?	What can you do differently next time?

Compassion in exposure

For exposure to be successful, it is important that you feel safe and develop ways to 'soothe' your overactive threat system. This may be internally, for example having the ability to self-soothe, to be understanding and non-judgemental, and encouraging yourself to approach difficult situations. If this is not possible, there may need to be someone with you who can help to soothe you, someone who is emotionally supportive and encourages you to approach difficult things and tolerate the distress. This is an entirely different approach to trying to be rational and reassuring yourself why you will not vomit. In order to develop these skills, it might be helpful to do some extra reading and practice on self-compassion. We recommend *The Compassionate Mind Workbook* by Elaine Beaumont and Chris Irons, published by Robinson (2017). It provides an introduction and overview of the approach, with lots of helpful exercises to follow for the interested reader.

Anna's experience of exposure

In line with her goals, Anna decided to work on her avoidance of food, catching an illness and her control over her son Adam's behaviour. She made a list of different situations that made her feel anxious, using the table. She included her SUDs ratings of how anxious each one would make her, and put them in order using a graded exposure hierarchy (0 = no distress, 100 = overwhelming distress). Anna felt very nervous about the first item in her hierarchy. However, she knew she had to start somewhere, and chose this first because it felt achievable with her husband Tom's support.

Planned exposure task	SUDs rating (0–100)
Eating a meal that my husband cooks without going into the kitchen or telling him what to cook in advance.	50
Eating a chicken roast with my family without checking if it's cooked or how my tummy feels afterwards.	50
Eating at the local Indian restaurant without checking the menu or the hygiene rating before I go.	60
Eating a larger portion at dinner time so I feel full without taking anti-nausea medication, seeking reassurance or checking how my tummy feels.	70
Letting Adam play at the park with other children without moving him away, checking how my tummy feels or asking him how he feels.	90
Letting Adam go to a children's party and eating whatever he wants, without asking how he feels.	90
Letting Adam go to nursery even if I know that other sick children will be there.	95
Visiting my grandmother in hospital and making an effort not to wash my hands, seek reassurance or check how my tummy feels.	100

She asked him to make her a meal of his choice and they agreed she would stay in the living room while he cooked. They sat down to eat the meal together, and with Tom's support she was able to keep her attention focused on the conversation instead of whether she felt nauseous. She made every effort not to reassure herself or use her safety phrases in her head to stop herself from getting ill. She also agreed with Tom that he would not answer her if she repeatedly asked him how he was feeling during the meal. Instead, he would hold her hand and ask her about her day. At first, Anna was very anxious and rated her anxiety at 80 per cent. However, with Tom's support and by focusing on the taste of the food, she found that gradually she was able to tolerate the situation. The more she ate and stayed with it, the better she started to feel. After 30 minutes, she noticed that she was feeling much less anxious and started to enjoy the meal. That evening she managed to finish half the meal and to her surprise she was not ill the next day.

This gave Anna the confidence to try to eat new foods and to go to the local Indian restaurant to keep building on her success. Gradually she started to vary her diet, and increased her portion sizes. She tried to push herself to do at least one task from her hierarchy every day. When she felt anxious, she vowed to 'stick with it' and tried hard to stay engaged in what she was doing instead of letting her attention focus on her body. She gained more confidence to stop using her mental rituals, and to reduce her cleaning.

Anna then decided to jump around the hierarchy and went straight to allowing her son to play with other children and eat what he wanted in many different contexts. She realized that if she stuck with it and remained focused, she could tolerate her anxiety and eventually it started to get less and less. Over time, she built a sense of resilience and a feeling that she could cope with the anxiety. Eventually, she went to see her grandmother and felt very proud that she could overcome her fear enough to support someone she loved. Anna felt that her life had opened up as she started to avoid things less and less. She realized she didn't need to engage in her safety-seeking behaviours as she could cope with feeling anxious without them. She then moved on to practising vomiting. She listened to sounds of vomiting, engaged with smells of vomit and did a role play of vomiting with her therapist.

Anna kept a record of her exposure tasks, which enabled her to keep track of her learning and plan what to do for the next task.

Exposure task	When/where	What did you learn?	Did you notice any subtle coping strategies?	What can you do differently next time?
Tom cooking dinner for me.	Tuesday evening. At home.	By focusing on the meal and conversation, I was able to tolerate it and I did not vomit.	I was slightly focused on my tummy after the meal.	Do it again, eating something different and making sure I fully engage in something different during and after the meal.
Tom cooking a different meal.	Thursday evening. At home.	I was able to enjoy this more the second time, especially by focusing on other things during and after, and again I was able to cope and did not vomit!	None.	Go to the local Indian restaurant for dinner.
Eat at our local Indian restaurant with Tom and a friend.	Sunday evening. Restaurant.	I was a lot more nervous but I managed to stick with it and it wasn't as bad as I expected.	I maybe chose a 'safer' meal than I could have done.	Try more adventurous foods.
Let Adam play in the park with his friend.	Monday. Park.	I was initially trying to control where they played but I stopped doing this and tried to focus on how much fun he was having and then I relaxed and enjoyed it.	I cleaned both our hands thoroughly when we got home.	Stop hand washing!

Exposure task	When/where	What did you learn?	Did you notice any subtle coping strategies?	What can you do differently next time?
Let Adam eat with the other children at Sophie's birthday party.	Wednesday. Local activity centre.	This time I really let go. I was busy talking to other mums and when I was engaged I felt much better, plus Adam did not get sick at all even though he ate so much! He looked as if he had a really nice time too.	None.	Keep repeating.
Go and see grandma in hospital.	Friday evening. Hospital	I was really anxious for this one but by staying with it and not asking Tom for reassurance, I found I was able to tolerate it without my usual behaviours.	None.	Next: fake vomit.

Working with the content of your thoughts

One core component of CBT is to use techniques to shine a spot-light on the content of your thoughts, and to test these out to see if they fit with Theory B. In emetophobia, we know it can be difficult to challenge thoughts about vomiting. Often people with emetophobia are unable to explain exactly what it is about vomit-ing that they are afraid of except for an extreme sense of awfulness if it were to happen. We often hear people say 'I would rather die than vomit', but they are unable to explain why or what it is about it that is particularly hard. We understand that reducing this sense of awfulness and not knowing whether you are going to vomit is extremely challenging. It is common for people with emetophobia to understand rationally that vomiting in itself is not threatening. However, when faced with specific situations, the anxious part of their brain is skilled at taking over and ensuring they avoid the risk of vomiting at all costs. Often the brain mistakenly misinter-prets the way you feel emotionally and physically in a situation as evidence that it is bad. For example, if you feel very scared about something, the brain makes an assumption that it must be very threatening and should be avoided, when in reality it is not. This is called 'emotional reasoning' – because you feel anxious then it must be a threat. This can be very powerful in emetophobia. This type of reasoning can make it hard to access the logical and rational parts of your brain when you are feeling anxious.

A key issue is learning to accept that you do not know whether you will vomit and to give up trying to control your vomiting. Trying to achieve 100 per cent certainty in knowing whether you are going to vomit, and attempting to control your body, are both impossible and make you more anxious. Try instead to focus on what you can control in your life by structuring your day, getting up at a regular time, eating regularly and connecting with friends and family without discussing the risk of vomiting. Make sure you do not keep checking for more information about norovirus alerts as this increases your sense of uncertainty and not being in control.

For these reasons, the emphasis is more on the 'doing' part of therapy, with the right attitude, when overcoming your emetophobia. This means tolerating not knowing whether you are going to vomit, accepting that vomiting is bearable and that you have little control over whether you vomit or not. Yes, if you had enough money you could live in a sterile bubble, but this has many unintended consequences.

It is important to understand the processes involved in maintaining your difficulties and committing to act against these in order to learn to tolerate uncomfortable emotions and body sensations. If you are able to accept Theory B on a rational level, but do not 'feel' it emotionally, then it is important to act 'as if' you already 'feel' the new idea. Over time, and with continued practice, you should find that your heart catches up with your head in learning that Theory B is the better explanation for your difficulties.

Behavioural experiments

We will outline the techniques involved in behavioural experiments, as they can still be helpful in emetophobia despite the emphasis on exposure. A behavioural experiment involves testing out each of your theories and investigating whether your experiences best fit with Theory B. In emetophobia, behavioural experiments can be used to learn more about your predictions, and to show the problem is you being fearful and worrying about vomiting, and that trying to make yourself certain about whether you are going to vomit and control everything around you makes it worse (Theory B).

For example, an experiment might involve eating chicken without overcooking it and then checking to see how your tummy feels during and after eating it. This will allow you test out whether this leads to losing control and more certainty (Theory A) or if the problem is that you are extremely worried about this and are too focused on preventing it (Theory B). Behavioural experiments can also help you to learn more about the processes that maintain your emetophobia, for example what effect does focusing on your body sensations have on your anxiety?

Below is a behavioural experiment worksheet for you to record your experiments. In the first column, write down any specific Theory A predictions you want to test out. In the second column, write down what you plan to do to test this out. Remember that you must commit to dropping any safety-seeking or maintaining strategies during the experiment. In the third column, write down exactly what happened after you completed the experiment. In the fourth column, record what you have learned from doing the experiment. Which theory is a better fit for your experience?

What is the thought or prediction?	What will you do to test it out?	What happened? How accurate were your predictions?	Is there a new way of thinking about the situation now? What else can you do to further test this out?

Ideas for experiments in emetophobia

To test out beliefs around control of vomiting

The next time you are feeling nauseous or bloated, try and make yourself vomit by thinking about it. Try as hard as you can to will yourself to be sick, or to imagine yourself vomiting, and see what happens.

To test out beliefs around the reactions of others

If you are worried that vomiting in front of others will lead to judgement or rejection, you can design a survey to give to others. Make your predictions first about what others might think or how they might react, and then ask other people questions such as how repulsive they would find it if someone vomited, how long they would feel repulsed, what they might think of that person or how they might react. Sometimes people may have experienced actual situations where someone has vomited, and you can ask them what it was like in relation to your specific predictions. A good therapist might go out with you and recreate vomiting in say a shopping centre to see what happens.

Jon's behavioural experiment

Jon decided to design a behavioural experiment to test his predictions about other people's reactions to someone vomiting in public. He remembered a traumatic experience of vomiting when he was young, when his parents reacted angrily. This appeared to be driving his main fear that others would judge him negatively for vomiting, and might respond angrily or reject him. He planned the below experiment to test out the accuracy of his anxious predictions.

What is the thought or prediction?	What will you do to test it out?	What happened? How accurate were your predictions?	Is there a new way of thinking about the situation now? What else can you do to further test this out?
If my friend pretends to vomit in public, then passers-by will notice and react to him angrily.	My friend will pretend to be sick outside a busy shopping centre. I will stand at a distance and watch how other people react. I will know if others are reacting badly if they move away, look angry or disgusted, or say something angrily to him.	Most people did not even notice, they kept walking and went about their day as usual. Not one person looked angry or disgusted, and no one shouted at him or told him off. Two people went up to him to ask if he was okay; they were very kind and seemed concerned for him.	Perhaps my predictions about what other people will think and do are not very accurate. It's possible that most people would react very differently from how my parents did. I could plan a survey to test this further.

Working with images

The way we think about a past or future situation can be in either spoken or picture form. Images or 'pictures' in the mind's eye that relate to a distressing past experience or an imagined future scenario of vomiting can be very powerful and distressing. Research shows that, in many cases, distressing images after an episode of vomiting can contribute to a person developing emetophobia. Therefore, it is important that we think about how to work with these.

Changing the distressing image

One way to work with distressing and unhelpful images of vomiting is to update the image so it loses its sense of 'nowness'. Try to make images as concrete and as humorous as possible. You can do this by sitting down comfortably, slowing your breathing down and letting the image come to mind. Ask yourself how this image might need to change to be less scary. Could you turn the image into something funny or silly? Perhaps someone could come into the image and help you. Often the image in our mind's eye stops at the very worst point in the experience. One option is to practise letting the scenario play out until you reach a point of safety. When you experience the distressing image again, practise calling to mind what happened next – when the distress is over, when you felt better or when someone had helped, and you felt safe. Have a go at playing with the image in your imagination and seeing what might be helpful for you. Alternatively, you could experiment with drawing or painting the image to make it concrete and less threatening.

Imagery re-scripting

Imagery re-scripting is a technique that can be used to overcome distressing images from early experiences of vomiting. The technique encourages you to close your eyes and talk about the experience as if it is happening to you again now. You describe the experience in detail in the first person and present tense, almost like describing a frame-by-frame movie: 'I am walking down the hallway and I start to feel sick.' You then focus on what your younger self needed at the time. It might be a hug from a loved one, or for someone to reassure or help you. The next phase involves imagining the same experience but as your adult self. Your adult self helps your child self and does exactly what the child needs until all their needs at the time are met. The third and final phase involves re-imagining the experience as the child and experiencing your adult self coming into the memory to help you. You imagine the experience until your adult self has done everything they can to help you and you feel calm and safe.

Imagery re-scripting helps to process past memories of vomiting as it allows you to experience the unwelcome thoughts and emotions you felt at the time, instead of avoiding them. It works towards reducing the 'sense of nowness' related to these images as it helps to time stamp the memory as something that happened in the past.

This technique is most helpful if you are troubled by images from past experiences of vomiting. It may not be relevant for everyone with emetophobia. These techniques may be best used with the support of a trained professional. If you are currently in therapy or are considering therapy, then it may be helpful to ask your therapist about re-scripting distressing images from the past.

Changing your thinking style

So far in this chapter we have discussed ways to approach your feared situations to learn to tolerate anxiety. We have outlined techniques to purposefully engage in exposure tasks in order to test that your predictions fit with Theory B. Another way to tolerate anxious thoughts is to learn a different way to respond to your thoughts, images and feelings. Instead of looking at ways to change the content of the thoughts, you can learn ways to be less affected by them, so they have less of an impact on your behaviour and your life. This approach is called 'mindfulness'. We are not suggesting that mindfulness is a treatment for emetophobia, and it is not helpful to practise mindfulness when you feel anxious or panicky. However, in the long term, it might help you in paying less attention to your anxious thoughts and feelings. It encourages you to be in the present moment and teaches you to notice your thoughts and let them pass, instead of getting caught up in what they say. In order to let your thoughts pass, first you have to practise noticing them and then allowing them to be there without changing them or seeing them as good or bad. You can label them as just thoughts and feelings, but remember they can't hurt you if you don't let them.

Let's try a simple exercise in mindfulness to give you a flavour. Find a quiet spot away from distractions. Sit comfortably with your back straight, your feet flat on the floor and your hands resting gently on your lap. Close your eyes and start to slow down your breathing. Breathe deeply and slowly through your nose and out through your mouth. Start to imagine a beautiful stream that is flowing beside you. Imagine the sights and sounds around you. You may notice that different thoughts come up for you as you immerse yourself in this scene. Imagine these thoughts to be leaves floating on the stream. Allow them to be there and let them gently float away down the water. If you notice yourself getting drawn into any particular thoughts or sensations, that is fine and completely normal. Don't worry about it or beat yourself up. Just start to notice when different thoughts pop up for you, and gently allow them to float away like a leaf on the stream.

This technique can be tricky to get the hang of at first, especially if your mind is busy or you feel very anxious. It often requires regular practice over a long period of time, and treating yourself with patience and compassion. And remember, the key to any mindfulness is not to block out or control your thoughts, but to allow them to be there and let them pass without judgement.

Reassurance seeking

As we know from Chapter 2, it is common for people with emeto-phobia to reassure themselves and to seek reassurance from others. Reassurance is a type of checking behaviour. It is important here to make a distinction between *assurance* and *reassurance*. For exam-ple, you might find it helpful to ask for help from a friend about something you are worrying about or tell yourself that things will be okay (assurance). However, if this becomes excessive, or you find yourself repeatedly seeking certainty about the same content, then this is likely to be reassurance and will make you even more anxious. We suggest instead that you seek emotional support from loved ones instead of reassurance. This might be asking for a hug, or talking about how you feel over a cup of tea.

The first step to changing any behaviour is to notice that you are doing it. You can start by making a mental note or a diary of problematic behaviours so that you become more aware of when and how often you are doing it.

A diary might look something like this:

Behaviour	Mon	Tues	Wed	Thur	Fri	Sat	Sun
Asking for reassurance	✓	✓ ✓		✓ ✓	✓		✓ ✓ ✓

Once you have noticed that you are doing a behaviour, you can stop yourself when it happens and then commit to doing something else. In terms of reassuring yourself, it might be helpful to focus your attention on something else. If you are seeking reassurance from someone else, it can be helpful to make the other person aware of this, and what it looks like, and to agree with them an alternative way to respond. A loved one may struggle not to give you reassurance, so it's important to explain that it keeps the problem going and there are better alternatives in the long term. This might be emotional support such as giving you a hug, holding your hand or making you a cup of tea as opposed to providing reassurance. It is helpful to have these conversations and come to an agreement with close friends and family when you are feeling calm, as you might both agree initially, but when you are anxious you might really want the reassurance you seek, and it might initially be hard if the other person does not give it to you. Therefore, it is important that you both agree (perhaps in writing) how to manage this before it happens.

Working with attention

When we are afraid of something, it is natural that our mind concentrates on what we fear so that we know how to react to keep ourselves safe. In emetophobia, our attention is trained to focus on things within ourselves and our environment that may represent risk. This might be self-focused attention (monitoring or noticing feelings of nausea or discomfort), or hypervigilance (being on the lookout for signs of danger in the external environment, such as signs of illness in others). The problem arises when our attention becomes overly focused on these signs of danger. This makes us very anxious, almost as if we are always looking out for the next thing that could cause harm. It also keeps us invested in the idea that we need to be careful, and reinforces the idea that vomiting is dangerous. Therefore, it is unhelpful and maintains the fear. We can therefore try to 'retrain' our attention to take notice of a wider range of things. These might include positive, neutral and negative aspects of our world. The idea here is not to totally avoid focusing on potential risks, as this would not be possible. However, we want to introduce flexibility in the way our attention focuses on our internal and external worlds. In this way, we have more choice over what we attend to, and we may become less automatically drawn to what we perceive to be threatening.

We will now outline techniques to use to start to retrain your attention. These exercises should not be tried when you feel very anxious or panicky. Always start your practice when you are not anxious and gradually introduce more difficult situations.

Becoming aware of what is around you

The world is full of different sensory experiences: sights, sounds, colours, textures, tastes. We can use these to help us to become more focused on the present moment, and less attuned to cues we perceive to be dangerous. Start by sitting down comfortably away from distraction and close your eyes. Try to become aware of the sounds that you can hear around you. These might be inside or outside the room. Spend two full minutes noticing every sound you can hear. Focus on what the different sounds are like, and what your experience is of hearing them. If you notice that your attention starts to wander during this exercise, don't worry. Just gently guide your focus back to the task at hand.

You can do this with any sense you like. Often people find it easier to start with sounds, but it works well for any of the other senses, for example looking around the room at all the different things you can see.

Practise switching your attention

Once you have tried tuning in to the sights or sounds around you, the next part is training your attention to switch between different cues. For example, you might spend a few minutes turning your attention from one sound to another and back again. Spend the first minute absorbing yourself in the first sound, and then switch to the second one. After a minute, come back to the first sound or a third. The key skill you are trying to master here is the ability to switch your attention back and forth between different sounds. You are not aiming to have complete control over your attention, or to block other experiences out of your awareness. It is very normal for your attention to be drawn to other things such as worries or your to-do list. The skill here is noticing when that happens, and gently guiding your attention back to whatever sense you are tuning in to. Be kind to yourself at first. Learning a new skill is not easy, and it can take time to get the hang of it. If you find yourself getting frustrated, leave it for a while and come back to it at a better time.

Examples of attention retraining exercises

- Listen to some music and practise focusing on the different instruments you can hear.
- Pay attention to the different objects around you. What colours and textures can you see?
- Pick up several objects and pay attention to what it feels like to touch them. Notice the different textures and what they feel like in your hands.
- Go for a walk outside and pay attention to the sounds and what you can see around you.

Making the exercises count

Like any new skill, it takes practice to master this. We recommend practising these exercises daily for around five to ten minutes. It can be helpful to make it a part of your daily routine, perhaps when you brush your teeth or make a cup of tea. This may help to make the practice a habit, so you will be less likely to forget to do it. In the short term, stick with sights and sounds. It is important to learn to do this skill when you are calm. If you are anxious or tense, it will be harder to focus your attention away from potentially threatening cues or anxious thoughts. Once you begin to get better at switching your attention, and it becomes easier, the long-term goal is to be able to notice when you are tuning in to cues relevant to your emetophobia. As soon as you notice this, you will be able to gently switch your attention towards something less threatening. It takes a lot of time, practice and patience to be able to do this when you are feeling very anxious, but it will be worth it in the end. It can be helpful to keep a diary of your daily practice using the worksheet below.

Day	What did I focus my attention on?	Where did I practise? E.g. inside/ outside	How long did I practise for?	Any other comments or learning

Working with worry

People with emetophobia often spend a lot of time worrying. This can be about many things such as nausea and internal discomfort, the risk of vomiting associated with various activities, illness, cleanliness, food hygiene. The list is endless. Often you can spend hours worrying and not even realizing you are doing it. In our vicious flower model, we can see that worrying is not a helpful activity as it keeps us preoccupied with a sense of threat in relation to vomiting. It also reinforces the message that there is something to worry about because vomiting is 'dangerous'. Even though it is a mental activity, worrying is a *behaviour* and as such we can choose whether we do it or not. This might sound impossible – you may feel that you have no control over your worrying or that it would be difficult to stop. However, it is possible to gain awareness of worry and when you do it, and then try to choose to do something different.

First, it is important to understand a little bit more about worry as a process. Worries tend to be repetitive thoughts about future scenarios: 'Maybe I won't pass my exams.' 'Will I be successful at my job interview?' 'What if I vomit during the meeting in front of my colleagues?' Worrying tends to look like lots of 'what if'-type thoughts that can make you feel anxious and on edge. Worrying is different from problem solving, because we often tend to worry about situations that are outside our control. Worry is therefore a process of trying to increase certainty or control over something that we do not know and have no control over. Therefore, even though we might be engaging in worry because we think it might help, it rarely does. In fact, it usually makes us more anxious or preoccupied about a problem.

Changing your behaviour around worry may seem hard at first, but it is achievable. The key is to first notice when you are worrying. Think about the following 'red flags' of worry and try to raise your awareness of when you worry so you can catch it early:

- Is there a time of day you typically worry more, such as before sleep?
- How do you feel when you are worrying?
- What are the signs you might be worrying?
- Are you asking yourself lots of 'what if' questions?

Once you have become more aware of when you are worrying, it can be helpful to understand the nature of your worries. What is it that you typically worry about? Write down ten of your most recent worries in the space below.

List of worries

Now look at the statements below and decide which one describes each of your worries. Put the number 1, 2 or 3 next to your worries in your list.

1. Worry about a situation that has not happened, and is outside your control.
2. Worry about a situation that could happen, but is outside your control.
3. Worry about a situation that could happen, and you can control.

How many of your worries were 1, 2 or 3? Did you notice that you had mostly one type of worry, and if so, which one was it? It is very common for people to mostly have worries that fit into description 1 – that is, worries about situations that have not happened, and even if they did, you would have little control over them anyway. This is especially relevant in emetophobia, as there tends to be a perception of control over vomiting. This leads to safety-seeking behaviours and positive beliefs about worry: 'If I worry about it then I can prepare for it and it will then be less likely to happen.' However, we know that in fact if we really needed to vomit then there would be little we could do about it, because vomiting is nature's way of protecting our bodies from harm. Therefore, worrying about it does not make any difference to the outcome, except make you more anxious and your emetophobia worse!

So, now you have noticed and defined your worries, let's think about what you can now do to stop unnecessary worries. Use the following diagram to help you decide what to do next.

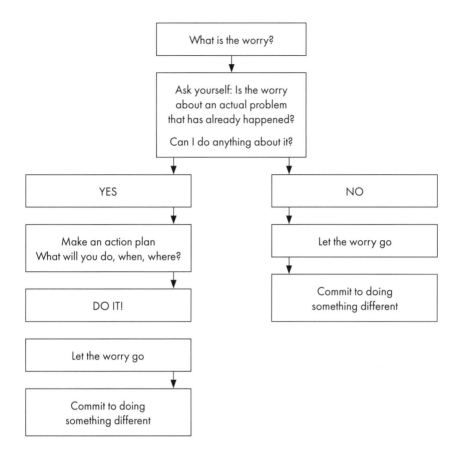

Committing to doing something different

In our experience, this is most likely to work if you choose an activity that is engaging and takes up mental energy. Some people find that it is too easy to go back to worrying if they are doing something familiar that does not require concentration. Here are some ideas of things to try:

- Speak to a friend.
- Engage in physical activity – go for a walk or do some exercise.

- Learn a new skill – knitting, a musical instrument, a new language.
- Test your brain by doing a puzzle or a crossword – something that needs thinking about is the best way to keep you on track and away from worrying.

Can you turn it into an experiment?

It can be helpful to design an experiment to test out your beliefs about worry. This might involve spending five minutes worrying about a problem, and then five minutes committing to doing something else. You can use the behavioural experiment worksheet outlined earlier in the chapter to help you. Afterwards you might want to think about the following questions:

- Were your beliefs about worrying accurate?
- How did the worrying make you feel compared to not worrying?
- Did worrying have any impact on the outcome of the problem?
- What have you learned about worry from this experiment and has it made you think about what you might like to do now in relation to worry?

Turn worry into preparation for vomiting

In emetophobia, worry will often be about future scenarios of vomiting. Another way to overcome worrying is to use the time to prepare yourself for vomiting in the future. Here it will be important to change 'what ifs' into a concrete and specific action plan – for example, like a fire drill or a job interview. Instead of spending time worrying about it, practise for it! This will involve a degree of acceptance that vomiting is likely in the future, instead of putting all your efforts into avoiding it at all costs. You may find it easier to tolerate the uncertainty or lack of control if you can invest your time in preparing for vomiting to happen, instead of going to extreme lengths to prevent it. This might involve all the exposure we have discussed (e.g. sounds and pictures of vomiting, fake vomit and role-playing). Try role-playing vomiting with a friend or therapist.

Chapter summary

- Exposure to feared situations and activities is the key component of CBT for emetophobia.
- Graded and repeated exposure can help you to learn to tolerate anxiety and uncertainty around vomiting.
- It is important to drop any safety-seeking behaviours and focus your attention externally during exposure.
- Working with images can be a helpful way to deal with distressing images from past experiences of vomiting.
- Seeking emotional support from close family and friends can be a good alternative to reassurance seeking.
- Attention exercises might give you more flexibility and choice over what you focus on, and avoid you being overly drawn to threat.
- Instead of worrying about vomiting, prepare yourself for it.

———

CHAPTER 6

Understanding and Dealing with Common Obstacles to Overcoming Emetophobia

Encountering obstacles at any point in your recovery from emetophobia is common and completely normal. The process of change is rarely straightforward and it is natural to experience ups and downs along the way. The important thing is to try not to avoid obstacles. It is better to recognize and face any potential difficulties and make a plan as to how you might overcome them.

You might find that you experience obstacles at different points in your recovery. It might be hard to get started, to stay on track during your recovery journey or to maintain progress in the long term. The key is to understand these obstacles, as this is the first step in overcoming them. This chapter talks about the many possible challenges you may face in your journey to overcoming your emetophobia. It is not a complete list, as some obstacles may be unique to you, but we have tried to include all the common ones that we see in our experience as therapists.

Trying too hard to be perfect

Many people can become convinced that there is a 'right' way to recover from their difficulties. After all, going through the hard and potentially painful process of facing your fears is only worth it if it is done correctly and has the most chance of success, right? This might be spending a lot of time researching the 'right' treatment, finding the 'best' therapist or treatment service, buying the 'best' self-help book and so on. However, the stronger your drive to get things 'right' or to do things in the 'best' possible way, the more risk there is of overthinking things and becoming anxious, which may end up slowing you down.

In trying to understand your difficulties, you might want to spend a lot of time getting to grips with every detail of your childhood, or every thought or feeling you may experience. While having a good understanding is certainly helpful, try to aim for a 'good enough' grasp of what is keeping your emetophobia going. Instead of striving to achieve the very 'best' thing, aim to just make a start. Anything you can do to make a start in doing exposure is often enough to gain a better understanding of your difficulties and is a good enough first step.

It is also important to avoid falling into the trap of aiming for a 100 per cent 'cure' of your emetophobia, as this is most likely impossible. Instead, we are aiming for you to be less impacted by your fears; going from a debilitating phobia to a manageable fear; to be able to accept some likelihood of vomiting in the future; and to be able to live your life exactly how you want despite this. It is very probable that you will still feel anxious about vomiting in future, and that if you were to vomit you would find it unpleasant. What we are aiming for is not for you to love the idea, but to be able to tolerate it just enough that you can live a life that is meaningful to you.

Fear of making things worse

This is a common and natural worry that many people face before they start any efforts to overcome emetophobia. You may have relied on your coping mechanisms and avoidance for a long time and as such they make you feel safe. You might also worry that any changes to these will put you at more risk of vomiting in the future, which naturally at this point you will want to avoid at any cost. Although this is understandable, research and our experience show that people with emetophobia are at no more risk of vomiting than people without emetophobia. It is important to note here that although people with emetophobia might recall episodes of vomiting more readily, there is in fact no difference in the rates of vomiting between people with emetophobia and those without the condition. This suggests that everything you are currently doing to avoid vomiting is not that successful at actually preventing it (even if it feels as if it is). We, as the authors of this book, for example, take no excessive precautions to avoid vomiting and have not vomited for many years. When one of us last went to India, we did not eat salads, drink unbottled water or eat from street vendors and only ate from restaurants that looked 'clean'. However, this is just standard advice for a tourist to avoid an upset stomach, and not a sign of excessive precautions.

Therefore, in everyday situations, the risk of vomiting is the same whether you do all your avoidance and safety behaviours or not. We also know from many years of treating people with emetophobia that the chances of therapy making your emetophobia worse are very small. The only outcome we can predict with any degree of certainty, therefore, is that by not making any changes to your approach and the way you act, your emetophobia will continue to cause you distress and interfere in your life until you die. It might improve a bit over time but it will not go away unless you do something about it.

Fear of looking back and regretting change

You may feel that the way you are living your life now is not that bad, and if you make changes then you might not like where you end up. Sometimes the certainty of knowing what to do and how to live with emetophobia is better than the alternative of not knowing what life might look like without it. People can feel very safe in their behaviours and ways of thinking, especially if they have been living a certain way for a long time. Change requires courage, and it is important to be sure why you are thinking of making the change in the first place. Remind yourself what it is about your life with emetophobia that brings you dissatisfaction. You might want to return to Chapter 3 and revisit the pros and cons of change to help you.

It can be helpful to cast your mind forward to the end of your life. Imagine that you have reached your 100th birthday and are reflecting on the life you have lived. Ask yourself what it is that you want that life to look like. What would you want your relatives to think of you and remember about you? What would you regret more: a life with or without trying to stop yourself vomiting?

Life is not without risks, and unfortunately no one can ever give you absolute certainty that those risks will be worth it. However, reaching your goals often takes a leap of faith and you can't know if you'll be happy until you get there. The only certainty is that your life will remain the same as it is now if you don't invest in something different.

Wanting coping mechanisms and techniques – the agenda of control

When you feel very anxious about something like vomiting, it is understandable that you will want to develop ways to cope. People often come to therapy wanting to arm themselves with all sorts of techniques to help them to manage their anxiety. The difficulty with this is that people can mistake coping mechanisms with safety-seeking behaviours. The intention, therefore, to develop such techniques to better avoid vomiting can at times be at odds with what therapy hopes to achieve. In CBT, the aim is to support people to face their anxiety and to *drop their usual coping mechanisms* in order to tolerate distress and accept that vomiting is possible. Therefore, if people hope to develop better safety-seeking behaviours that enable them to better control their fear or the likelihood of vomiting, then this can act to keep the emetophobia going rather than overcoming it.

For therapy to be successful, it is important to learn to tolerate uncertainty and discomfort, and that will involve accepting that you do not have control over vomiting. This means facing your anxiety head on without the use of safety-seeking and avoidance behaviours that enable your emetophobia to thrive.

Shame and self-criticism

A common obstacle to change can be strong feelings of shame. This can make it difficult to open up about your difficulties in the first place. You might struggle to share the progress of your recovery with others. People with emetophobia often have a strong inner critic who puts them down or tells them that there is no point. Your inner critic may try and convince you that you are to blame for having the problem in the first place, or for experiencing difficulties in overcoming your emetophobia. This can lead to even stronger feelings of shame. Remember, it is never your fault that you have emetophobia, and you are not alone. We know that trying to face this problem is incredibly difficult. It takes a lot of strength and courage to even try. So, it is important to be kind to yourself in the process. Allowing your inner critic to bully you is rarely helpful and may delay your progress.

One way to deal with your inner critic is to develop a compassionate voice that might help to soothe you or your critical voice. This compassionate voice is like a cheerleader who offers you encouragement and praise when you try. It can help you to recognize and celebrate the small wins, and keep you going when times are hard. The first step to developing your compassionate voice is to become more aware of when your critical voice is talking, and then to practise using your compassionate voice instead. Many people find this hard to do at first, as being kind to ourselves rarely comes naturally or easily. Ask yourself what you would say to a friend in a similar situation. Can you say the same kind of things to yourself? This is a helpful technique to start to build a compassionate voice for yourself. It may take effort to begin with, but the more you practise, the easier it will become.

Use the following worksheet to reflect on the experience of your critical voice, and to start to build up your compassionate voice. Don't worry if you find it hard to think about your compassionate voice to begin with, as this is very common. Keep practising using your compassionate voice, and eventually it will become louder.

Critical voice	Compassionate voice
In which situations does this voice tend to speak up?	In which situations does this voice tend to speak up?
What does this voice sound like? How does it speak to you?	What does this voice sound like? How does it speak to you?
What does this voice say to you?	What does this voice say to you?
Does it remind you of anyone?	Does it remind you of anyone?

Anna's critical and compassionate voices

Anna was finding exposure tasks difficult to face, as she was beating herself up about feeling anxious and not being able to pull herself together. She had always been self-critical and did not remember ever experiencing compassion from others. She knew that she had to develop a compassionate voice in order to be kind and encourage herself to face her fears. She filled in the worksheet below, which helped her to become more aware of her critical voice, and start to develop a compassionate voice to respond to it.

Critical voice	Compassionate voice
In which situations does this voice tend to speak up?	In which situations does this voice tend to speak up?
When I feel nauseous or anxious.	*If I think I have done something well.*
When I try to do an exposure task and it doesn't go well.	*When I am thinking of others or being kind to them, especially Adam.*
When I make mistakes.	
When I feel I'm not doing well enough as a partner or mother.	
What does this voice sound like? How does it speak to you?	What does this voice sound like? How does it speak to you?
It sounds harsh and judgemental.	*Soft, soothing, kind.*
It speaks in a direct and abrupt way.	*It speaks to me positively and encourages me.*
It sounds like an angry teacher telling me off.	*I recognize this voice more when I think about or speak to others.*
What does this voice say to you?	What does this voice say to you?
You are pathetic.	*You've done that well.*
You're not trying hard enough.	*You tried really hard.*
Pull yourself together and just get on with it.	*Good job, keep going.*
Your family would be better off without you.	*It's not your fault.*
	It will be okay.
Does it remind you of anyone?	Does it remind you of anyone?
Not really – maybe my parents.	*Tom, close friends.*

Intolerance of discomfort

We know that the emotional and physical elements of emetophobia are complex and can be devastating. Constant feelings of fear, panic, nausea and discomfort are extremely difficult to live with. It is very understandable therefore that people with emetophobia go to such lengths to avoid them. If you have been using safety-seeking behaviours and avoidance for a long time, then starting to act differently can bring on many feelings that you haven't experienced for some time. It is very common that people may find it hard to tolerate the discomfort that this can cause. This inability to tolerate discomfort may make it hard to even try the techniques we suggest.

We know that the first step in overcoming your difficulties is to allow yourself to be open to your distress instead of avoiding it. It may feel intolerable in the short term, but the more exposure you do, the easier it gets.

It is important to be clear here that by no means do we think your discomfort is not real or is easy to manage. We understand that for some it can be a huge struggle to even contemplate change. This is the reason we suggest starting out in a graded manner, starting with the smallest task first and building up your ability to tolerate discomfort gradually. Think of it like training to run a marathon. You wouldn't expect your body to be able to withstand the physical demands of running 26.2 miles straight away. You build up the distance gradually and over time, until your body has the stamina and physical ability to cope with long distances. It can be helpful to use the support of a trusted loved one here. Much like training with a running partner, having someone to motivate, encourage and support you initially can be beneficial.

Another possible strategy to use in overcoming intolerance of discomfort is mindfulness. This should not be offered as a sole treatment for emetophobia. We suggest that it may be helpful after you have recovered from emetophobia. This approach teaches us in the long term, after a lot of practice, to experience thoughts and emotions in the moment and without judgement. It can help us to change our relationship with difficult thoughts and emotions. Instead of us trying to avoid them or control them, mindfulness allows them to be there as passing events. This is a technique that requires regular daily practice, and the use of popular apps or guided exercises can be helpful.

Not enough time

CBT is an approach that emphasizes the importance of 'doing' and 'acting' differently. It takes time and commitment to make these changes. Sometimes it can feel as if you don't have enough time to fully commit to practising every day. In our experience, the more people are able to put into this approach in their everyday life, the more they get out of it. Perhaps it would be helpful to revisit your goals and think about why you are investing in making these changes. What does the future look like without emetophobia? What will you be able to do in the future that you cannot do now and what will this mean to you? It might be helpful to make a list of all your current commitments and work out if any can be put on hold for the time being while you prioritize your mental health and well-being. Are there ways you can make changes to your schedule so that you can make time for this work?

With that said, we understand that overcoming your emetophobia is not at all easy. It takes hard work and commitment. You might decide that now is simply not the best time in your life to start due to other stressors that cannot be put off. If this is the case, then it may be best to give yourself some time and come back to it when you can give it your full attention.

Insufficient dose of deliberate practice

In Chapter 5, we outlined why deliberate and planned exposure is crucial in overcoming your fears. If you are finding it hard to get started, it might be helpful to re-read this again, to ensure you have a good understanding of why it is important. Pay attention to any thoughts that might be getting in the way of exposure tasks. Write these down and ask yourself how best to test these out. If you find that a particular task is too difficult, can you go back down the hierarchy and choose something that is more manageable? Even if you have to repeat tasks that may be easy, this will help to build your confidence and practise feeling the anxiety subside in feared situations.

Exposure is not frequent enough

The most important part of overcoming your emetophobia is the 'doing' part; that is, practising facing your fears and learning to tolerate your anxiety without using safety-seeking behaviours or avoidance. The more often you practise, the quicker you are likely to see change. We would suggest that you try to engage in one exposure task every day as a minimum. It can be helpful to plan exposure into your daily routine by setting aside a specific time that you will do it and then sticking to it. When working your way up the hierarchy, it can be unhelpful to leave a long gap between each exposure task. This can make the anxiety build before doing the next one and you might think yourself out of doing it. Much like ripping off a plaster, it is most helpful to just get on with it without thinking about it too much. You might also benefit from using the confidence you gain from early success to help you to tackle the next task in your hierarchy. Think of it like riding a bicycle: the speed you get from going down a hill can help you to get up the next one!

Exposure tasks are not long enough

Exposure tasks must be long enough for you to really tolerate the anxiety and to practise a different way of coping. You need to stay in your feared situation for longer so that you can learn to tolerate discomfort. Only then will it get easier when you repeat the activity. The aim is to engage in activities that cause your anxiety to be as high as possible, and to do this for as long as you can tolerate. It is helpful to repeat the same exposure tasks again and see if your anxiety has reduced as much as it did the previous time. It is important that you stick with the feared situation without using safety-seeking behaviours or avoidance for long enough to show your brain that this was not just a 'lucky escape'. You need to give yourself enough of an opportunity so that there can be no doubt as to why your anxiety reduced or you could tolerate distress. Can you have a go at making your next exposure task longer and see what happens?

Using safety-seeking behaviours and reassurance during exposure

Go back to Chapters 2 and 5, and remind yourself why it is so important to fully drop your safety-seeking behaviours, reassurance seeking or being rational to yourself. This includes reassuring yourself mentally as much as seeking reassurance from others. Remember to seek emotional support and do not discuss vomiting. Try to be aware of the behaviours you need to resist doing and tell yourself why you are doing it. If you do happen to use a behaviour or reassurance, repeat the task as soon as possible making a mental note to resist doing it again next time. Remember that safety-seeking behaviours can be subtle, and you might not be aware you are using them. You might also be holding on to avoidance by not exposing yourself fully. Try to be as aware and as honest with yourself as possible. If an exposure task did not work, or you did not feel the anxiety subsiding, ask yourself if there was anything you were doing or saying to yourself that could have stopped this from happening. Write it down and try again.

Not taking up naturally occurring opportunities for exposure

In Chapter 5, we emphasized the importance of engaging in deliberate exposure and behaviour experiments. Initially, it is important to create opportunities to start to act differently and to do this at a comfortable pace. However, it is rare that you can plan every opportunity for exposure in advance and you may find yourself occasionally presented with golden opportunities to test out your thoughts or face your fears that you did not plan yourself. A friend may invite you out to lunch at a new restaurant at short notice, for example, or you might have to take a different route to work one day. These are opportunities to really test your progress, and to do the opposite of what your anxiety is telling you. It is, of course, unrealistic to think that you will be able to jump into every opportunity straight away, and it is also about being kind to yourself for trying new things big or small. However, in our experience we have found that those who allow themselves the most opportunities for exposure are often the ones who get the most out of treatment, and who see the biggest and most lasting changes. Often people report that these opportunities work out much better than expected. They have enabled learning and a sense of satisfaction, which may have otherwise been missed through avoidance.

Make a plan for overcoming your obstacles

You can use the worksheet below to note down your obstacles to progress and make a concrete and specific plan for how to tackle each one. Use recent examples that are fresh in your mind to give you something to work with. Make the plan as specific as you can, for example I will do this, and when, and with whom. You can come back to the sheet and make changes to the plans if needed.

Obstacle	Plan

Here is Sally's plan for overcoming her own obstacles:

Obstacle	Plan
Being worried about facing my fears, dropping my safety-seeking behaviours and feeling out of control.	Remind myself why I am making changes in the first place, revisit my goals and pros and cons of change and remember that I will only get better if I learn to tolerate anxiety and uncertainty.
	Use the worksheet to record my exposure tasks and make notes of any of these thoughts that could be getting in the way, and ask a friend to do the exposure with me.
Criticizing myself all the time.	Use the compassionate voice worksheet to start to develop a way to be kinder to myself. Ask myself what I would say to a friend in the same situation. Make a note of any critical thoughts and try to respond with compassion and kindness, and reward myself for trying, even if I don't get it 100 per cent perfect.
Not sticking with exposure tasks for as long as I need to.	Go back and read Chapter 5 to remind myself why this is important. Use breathing techniques to calm myself down. Ask a friend to help me to stay with it, and keep trying until I can manage it on my own.

Chapter summary

- Obstacles are a common and normal part of recovery.
- The key is to understand them and make a plan of how to overcome them.
- The most common obstacles we have outlined are:
  - trying to be perfect
  - fear of making things worse
  - fear of regretting change
  - wanting more techniques to control the fear and the likelihood of vomiting
  - intolerance of discomfort
  - shame and self-criticism
  - not having enough time to commit to change
  - difficulties with exposure.
- You may relate to some or all of these, or recognize your own obstacles that are unique to you.
- Make a plan for how you will tackle obstacles – and do it!

—

CHAPTER 7

Bringing it All Together

Monitoring your progress

Record your evidence for Theory B

As you put the techniques outlined in Chapter 5 into practice, you will be doing frequent exposure tasks and experiments in order to build evidence for Theory B. It is important to record your findings as you go along, so that you can refer to your evidence for a less threatening alternative explanation for your difficulties. This will help you to reflect on what you have learned and to make the most of the work you are doing. We have provided a worksheet for you to record your evidence below. First, write down what Theory B tells us about your difficulties, for example *The problem is that I am very fearful of vomiting, that I cannot know for certain whether I am going to vomit or not, that I can't bear it if I vomit and I am trying too hard to prevent myself from vomiting. My solutions of avoiding and checking make my problem worse.* Then after each exposure task and experiment, write down in the table how your experience best fits with this theory.

Theory B says:

Evidence for Theory B:

Re-rate your goals

You will remember in Chapter 4 that you set yourself SMART goals for the short, medium and long term. We recommend that you regularly monitor your progress with regard to these goals, using the SMART goals worksheet in Chapter 4 and on the SPOVI (also in Chapter 4). As you progress, you might find that you are making good headway with some goals, but not others. This might help to shape what you need to be working on next with your exposure tasks and experiments. Progress with your goals might be a good indication as to how you are doing overall, and how long you might need to continue using these techniques in a deliberate way.

How long do I need to do work on my emetophobia?

It is hard to determine exactly how long you might need to face your fears in a planned and deliberate way. Each person's experience is unique to them, and some may need to work on their difficulties for longer than others. We do know that the more time and effort you put in, the faster you are likely to see improvements. It is likely that you will need to continue to work on facing your fears to some degree indefinitely, in order to maintain your progress. For some people, it might be reasonable to expect significant improvement and a return to many activities that were previously avoided. However, for others it might be more realistic to expect that a manageable *fear* of vomiting (not a phobia) will remain a part of their life for the long term, but we would hope that it would have less of an impact on their daily activities. Either way, it is unrealistic to expect that a brief period of putting these approaches into practice will be sufficient to overcome your emetophobia in the long run. It is more likely that recovery will be a lifelong journey of continued practice and effort to maintain what you have achieved and learned as a result of acting in a different way.

At this stage, if you feel as if you have made good progress, it is important to consider what needs to happen in order to stay well. This is called 'relapse prevention' and we will think about this in more detail in the next section.

Next steps and maintaining progress

Once you feel you have made sufficient progress, it can be a useful exercise to think ahead to next steps and how to keep your successes going. A helpful place to start is to reflect on what was keeping your emetophobia going. You might want to refer back to Chapter 2 to help you with this. Think about your avoidance, excessive vigilance, worry, checking, reassurance seeking and avoidance behaviours.

What was keeping my emetophobia going?

. . . .

. . . .

. . . .

. . . .

. . . .

Once you have considered the processes that were keeping your emetophobia going, think about what you learned that was helpful in overcoming these. This might be from completing exposure tasks, behavioural experiments or any other techniques outlined in Chapter 5.

✳

What did I learn that was useful?

. . . .

. . . .

. . . .

. . . .

. . . .

. . . .

. . . .

Next, think about what you need to keep practising and keep your successes going. Some people find it helpful to plan further exposure tasks, or techniques to maintain progress. You might want to schedule a regular 'check in' with yourself every week to review how you are doing and things you need to practise. As times goes on, you may feel you need to do these less frequently as this work becomes second nature. Can you get a notebook or a folder to keep all techniques and learning in one place? Some find this a useful resource to come back to in the future.

✳

What do I need to keep working on?

. . . .

. . . .

. . . .

. . . .

. . . .

. . . .

. . . .

How to deal with a setback

It is important to acknowledge that setbacks to progress are very common, and a normal part of recovery. It is unrealistic to expect progress to be linear, and there will naturally be ups and downs moving forward. The more important part of maintaining progress is not whether you have a setback – as most people do – but *how you respond to them* and get yourself back on track. First, let's think about what you will need to look out for. How will you know that you are having a setback? This will look different for every person; however, it might be that you are feeling more anxious and some of your old strategies are slowly creeping back in. Have a think about any red flags that might be a sign that you are having a setback and write them in the space below.

What might be the signs of a setback?

. . . .

. . . .

. . . .

. . . .

. . . .

Next, think about what you need to do to respond. Who might you need to speak to for support? Can you look over your self-help resources or revisit relevant chapters to refresh your memory of helpful learning or techniques? Can you plan some exposure tasks or other techniques that could help you get back on track? Above all, remember to be kind to yourself. It is not your fault that this has happened. It is how you pick yourself up that is most important, and that will be much easier if you practise self-compassion rather than criticism. Think about who or what will help you and make some notes in the space below.

✱

What do I need to do to get back on track?

· ·

· ·

· ·

· ·

· ·

When to consider professional help

We hope that this book has provided a helpful first step in outlining the approaches necessary to overcome emetophobia. For some, self-help may be a useful way to learn more about difficulties, and how to make changes to live a life without fear. However, for many, self-help might be a useful addition to professional help. We want to acknowledge that emetophobia is a complex problem that can be difficult to treat. If you feel that you have given these approaches a try for a few months, yet your emetophobia remains a problem, we recommend you seek professional help. There is no shame in needing support from a trained professional, as so many with emetophobia do. We will talk more about the types of professional support available, and how to access these, in Chapter 9. Even if you had professional help, they may not have been following this protocol, and sometimes one needs a therapist who is more experienced in emetophobia. Ultimately, we need more research and funding in this area to learn how to best treat emetophobia. This requires political action and the support of charities that are trying to put emetophobia higher on everyone's agenda.

Chapter summary

- It is helpful to record all your evidence for Theory B in the worksheet provided as this will help you to reflect on your learning and make the most of your efforts.
- Remember to keep frequently re-rating progress towards your goals as this will help to shape what you work on and keep you on track.
- Continuing to put these techniques into practice over the long term is most likely to help you to maintain your gains.
- It might be more realistic that your phobia turns into a 'fear' of vomiting, as opposed to disappearing completely.
- When you feel ready, make sure you complete a 'relapse prevention plan' and make notes of what you have learned to help you plan how to recognize and deal with a setback.
- Remember that setbacks are common and not a sign of failure – it is how you respond to them that counts.
- If you find that your symptoms do not improve after a few months of trying self-help techniques, then you might benefit from seeking professional help.

CHAPTER 8

———

Medical Treatments for Emetophobia

Anti-nausea medication

Anti-nausea medication is often prescribed at the request of people with emetophobia. This includes drugs such as metoclopramide (trade name Reglan), prochlorperazine (Stemetil, Compazine) or domperidone (Motilium). However, the nausea in emetophobia is caused by anxiety! Anti-nausea drugs do not stop you being sick! Such drugs may take the edge off your anxiety or may act as a placebo in reducing nausea. A placebo is a substance that does not contain any medical ingredients and is often prescribed for psychological (instead of medical) benefit. Anti-nausea medication doesn't solve the problem and it is unhelpful in the long term as it strengthens the idea that you can stop yourself from vomiting. Therefore, anti-nausea medication is a safety-seeking behaviour – see Chapter 2. This gives you the illusion of control and certainty that you will not be sick. Anti-nausea medication needs to be stopped as part of therapy and has no place in overcoming emetophobia.

Selective serotonin reuptake inhibitors (SSRIs)

There is no medication licensed for treating emetophobia. There is some rationale for a type of medication called a selective serotonin reuptake inhibitor (or SSRI for short) in those with severe symptoms of emetophobia that overlap with obsessive compulsive disorder (OCD). However, this would normally be done after a good trial of CBT where the results have been mixed. SSRIs are likely to have limited benefit but may take the edge off your anxiety. In people with more moderate to severe OCD, the results may be as effective as CBT.

SSRIs act on serotonin nerve endings in the brain. 'Selective' refers to the fact that they act on serotonin nerve endings rather than others such as noradrenaline or histamine nerve endings. 'Reuptake inhibitor' refers to the way the drug acts – it helps to stop serotonin being taken back up into the nerve, increasing the amount of free serotonin available. This in turn helps to increase the messages passing along certain pathways in the brain, and to reduce anxiety. Cast your mind back to Chapter 2 where we described the causes of emetophobia and the threat system which is designed to keep you safe. So, the fear causes a large load on the system as another part of your brain desperately tries to reduce your anxiety. SSRIs probably restore *normal* brain activity to help to increase courage and support you to approach difficulties. SSRIs are widely used in the treatment of anxiety disorders and especially OCD. A family doctor may prescribe the drug. Therefore, most of the information below relates to how SSRIs are used in OCD, which can be similar to emetophobia.

On average, symptoms in OCD reduce by half with SSRIs. Some patients may get no benefit while others may become symptom free. Even if the medication is of benefit, it will not work right away. Most people notice some improvement in their symptoms after about four weeks, while maximum benefit should occur for most people within 12 to 16 weeks. *It is therefore important to continue to take your medication at the highest dose you can manage for at least 12 weeks before deciding if it is working.* When deciding this, always compare the score on a rating scale (see Chapter 4) before and after taking the drug. Ideally, take the drug when you are not receiving any CBT to judge how well it is working for you. Some people may continue to see improvement for several months before reaching a plateau.

All the SSRIs are equally effective in OCD, but any one person may respond better to one SSRI over another. The initial choice will depend on possible side effects or the personal preference of your doctor. If you or someone in your family did well or poorly with a medication in the past, this may influence the choice. If you have medical problems (e.g. with sleeping) or are taking another medication, these factors may influence your doctor's choice so that side effects and possible drug interactions are minimized. There are some differences between the SSRIs. For example, fluoxetine takes longer to be processed by the body. So, if you forget a dose one day, you can get away with it because some fluoxetine will stay in the blood if you stop taking it. It also tends to be easier to stop.

What dose of an SSRI should I be prescribed?

The normal starting dose and suitable target doses of the medication are listed in Table 8.1. If you can, it's important to try a higher dose, as a greater improvement is made with the higher doses. If you experience side effects, then you can always start on a lower dose and build it up slowly. The target dose for fluoxetine is listed below at 60mg because this is the maximum recommended in the

UK. However, in the USA and other countries the maximum dose is 80mg.

Table 8.1: SSRIs and potent SRIs (serotonin reuptake inhibitors) used for OCD

Chemical name	UK trade name	US trade name	Usual starting dose	Target dose	Liquid preparation
Citalopram	Cipramil	Celexa	20mg	40mg	Yes
Clomipramine	Anafranil	Anafranil	50mg	225mg	No
Escitalopram	Cipralex	Lexapro	10mg	20mg	Yes
Fluoxetine	Prozac	Prozac	20mg	60mg	Yes
Fluvoxamine	Faverin	Luvox	50mg	200mg	No
Paroxetine	Seroxat	Paxil	20mg	40mg	Yes
Sertraline	Lustral	Zoloft	50mg	200mg	Yes

What about SSRIs for a child or adolescent?

SSRIs have been studied quite well for children with OCD and are as effective as they are for adults. They are safe, although it is true that we don't yet know the long-term effects of such drugs on brain development in children. This possible risk needs to be judged against the risk of *not* using medication. This is especially true for a young person who has not responded to CBT (or has difficulty accessing it) and continues to experience OCD symptoms. If untreated, these may have a major impact on their development and education.

The dose for a young person is the same as that for an adult.

However, younger or smaller children usually start at a lower dose and increase gradually. Sertraline and fluvoxamine are licensed for use in young people with OCD in the UK. Sertraline and fluoxetine are licensed for young people in the USA. Licensing of a drug by a regulatory body means that the manufacturer has submitted data from clinical trials looking at specific problems (e.g. for OCD). This allows them to promote the use of their drug in that area. They all seem effective, so the doctor may choose an unlicensed one if they think it may suit the child better and it is agreed that this would be better for the child.

In general, the use of SSRIs for children should be supervised by a psychiatrist.

In summary, the authorities continue to recommend SSRIs for young people with OCD. The side effects listed below occur in children as they do in adults. In addition, children may become over-excited, irritable or silly. If this is severe, it may be a reason to stop the medication.

Will an SSRI have side effects?

Side effects of SSRIs depend on the dose of your medication and for how long you have been taking it. Most people experience minor side effects that usually decrease after a few weeks. These are not usually a problem for people who need to take a drug in the long term. The worst side effects usually occur in the first few days or weeks after starting the drug. This is the time when you are most likely to stop taking the drug because you have not seen any improvement in symptoms. (This is because it takes up to 12 weeks for the full benefits of the medication to become clear.) There is one side effect that does not tend to improve over time: sexual difficulties. We will discuss below how these might be improved. Side effects that do not improve over time, including sexual difficulties, will decrease when you stop taking the medication.

You are more likely to experience side effects if you are on a higher dose or if your dose has been increased quickly. If your side effects are too severe, you can try reducing the dose and then increasing it to the previous level more slowly. For example, if you find that you are experiencing headaches after a few days of taking fluoxetine 20mg, you can reduce the dose to 10mg (using the liquid form) for a week or two. You can then increase it to 20mg again when your body has become more used to the drug. If you are very sensitive to side effects your doctor may start you on a lower dose as a liquid and increase it very slowly. For example, you might start on 2mg of fluoxetine and increase this by 2mg per week. Another alternative is to switch to a different SSRI altogether.

Is there anything I can do to reduce side effects of SSRI medication?

We have listed below the most common side effects of SSRIs and how to deal with them. Most will go away after a few weeks and all of them will stop if you decide to stop taking the drug. This must be done slowly and under guidance from your doctor.

1. Nausea

Nausea (feeling sick) is the most common but *short-term* side effect of an SSRI. It affects about a quarter of patients taking an SSRI compared to about one tenth of those on a placebo. This is, of course, difficult for someone with emetophobia. However, it does not mean you are going to be sick; it just means you may *feel* sick. This may be helpful exposure to the feeling of nausea.

Nausea can be helped by taking the drug after food. Or you

can take half of the dose for a couple of weeks and then increase it slowly back to the normal dose. If the nausea is still a problem for you then it may help switching to a different SSRI. Nausea from SSRIs generally improves over time.

2. Diarrhoea or constipation

SSRIs cause diarrhoea in up to 15 per cent of patients taking an SSRI compared to about 5 per cent taking a placebo. For diarrhoea, always drink plenty of water or use rehydration sachets. Diarrhoea can be helped by drinking plenty of apple juice (which contains pectin). You can also use medications such as loperamide or bismuth subsalicylate (Pepto-Bismol). Remember that diarrhoea can also occur because of severe anxiety or feelings of disgust.

Constipation occurs in another 5 per cent of patients taking an SSRI. This may be improved by having plenty of fruit and fibre in your diet. If altering your diet does not help, then bulking agents such as Fybogel or medicines like lactulose or macrogol may help. For both diarrhoea and constipation, you should drink at least two litres of water a day.

3. Headache

Up to one fifth of patients taking an SSRI find they develop headaches. Headache is also a common symptom of tension and occurs in a small proportion of patients taking a placebo. Symptoms of headache can usually be helped by drinking water and taking simple painkillers such as paracetamol. Headaches should get better after a few weeks of taking an SSRI. Ibuprofen or similar anti-inflammatory drugs are not recommended with SSRIs as they can increase the risk of bleeding.

4. Excessive sweating

Excessive sweating occurs in about 10 per cent of patients taking an SSRI compared to 5 per cent taking a placebo. There is no easy solution to this problem, although it should get better over time. Remember that sweating may also be a feature of anxiety. You could try reducing the dose, but this may worsen your emetophobia. A low dose of an anticholinergic drug such as benztropine may be helpful for sweating.

5. Dry mouth

Dry mouth affects about 10 per cent of patients taking an SSRI compared with 5 per cent taking a placebo. Sucking on sugarless gum may stimulate production of saliva. You could try a spray or pastilles that can be bought over the counter to provide artificial saliva. Make sure you drink plenty of water. Again, the symptoms usually get better over time.

6. Tremor

Shakiness or tremor occurs in about 10 per cent of patients taking an SSRI and 3 per cent on a placebo. A beta-blocker (e.g. propranolol) may reduce tremor if it is severe.

7. Sedation or insomnia

Up to one fifth of people on an SSRI feel sedated and a smaller portion cannot sleep. The problem can sometimes be helped by changing the time of day you take your medication. You can take it at night, for example, if it makes you drowsy. Sometimes it might be better to take a different SSRI altogether. Fluvoxamine is more likely to cause sleepiness and may be best taken at night. Another solution may be to take a sedative drug to help you sleep in the short term.

8. Emotional numbness

This is a tricky one. Some people experience feeling emotionally numb or 'spaced out' on an SSRI. This potential side effect seems to be related to the dose, so a lower dose may improve things (but it may worsen the emetophobia). If you stop taking the drug, your feelings return to normal.

9. Sexual problems

Sexual side effects can take the form of delayed ejaculation in men and an inability to reach an orgasm in women. SSRIs can occasionally cause both men and women to lose their libido. However, this may be a result of the person having depression as well as anxiety. It might be helpful just to check testosterone levels. Adding testosterone gel can lead to improvement in sexual function in men with low or low to normal testosterone levels.

Sometimes the problem can be solved with a lower dose of medication, although this may make the emetophobia worse. Taking a once-a-week 'drug holiday' and skipping a dose before sexual activity may be helpful. However, some SSRIs lead to side effects if you do this (e.g. paroxetine). Missing the drug more than once a week risks the return of emetophobia symptoms. Omitting the drug will not stop loss of libido. Another option is to try an alternative SSRI but it may have the same effect. Sertraline, citalopram or escitalopram may be associated with fewer sexual problems than other SSRIs. It might be worth switching to one of these if another one is causing problems.

There is some evidence for the use of Viagra (sildenafil) or Cialis (tadalafil) for men and women to help with the side effect of not achieving an orgasm if taken regularly. The dose of Viagra is 50mg to be taken one hour before sexual activity. If this does not improve things, you could try increasing it to 100mg. Some patients with heart conditions will not be able to take it. The possible side effects of Viagra include headache, flushing and dizziness. Other case reports for improving sexual function have included adding another class of antidepressant to the SSRI, including trazodone (at a low dose of 100mg) or mirtazapine (at a low dose of 7.5–15mg) or buspirone (20–60mg a day) in both men and women or bupropion (20–60mg a day) in women. Trazodone or mirtazapine are best taken at night as they tend to increase sedation. It is not known how they may be beneficial.

There may be other factors linked to sexual problems, some of which may be possible to treat. These include the nature of your relationship, depression, alcohol and smoking.

10. Loss of appetite

Loss of appetite and weight loss occur in about 5 to 10 per cent of patients taking SSRIs. Reducing the dose can help, though it usually improves over time anyway. Some SSRIs can also cause mild weight gain in the long term. In this case, you may need to adjust your diet and exercise programme. Depression and inactivity will also contribute to weight gain.

11. Nervousness or agitation

Some people feel more anxious or 'wired' especially when starting an SSRI. It can be difficult to tell the difference between the anxiety that comes from emetophobia and that which might be caused by the drug. If it is caused by the drug then it may be solved by a) switching to a different SSRI, b) trying a lower dose, or c) adding an additional drug in the short term. The feeling of increased anxiety is usually temporary and will reduce over time. Rarely, the feeling of agitation can develop into an abnormal mood of elation or irritability. You may find your speech becomes fast, you feel as if you do not need any sleep and as if you are 'on the go' all the time. This is called a state of mania and you are likely to need to stop taking the SSRI.

Summary

Whenever side effects are a problem, always discuss them with your doctor. The doctor may advise you to a) reduce the dose, b) try a different SSRI, c) add another medication to counteract side effects such as insomnia or sexual problems, or d) wait and see, as many of the side effects improve over time.

If SSRI medication doesn't work, is there anything else I can try?

All SSRIs are equally effective overall, but one person may get a better response from one than another. If one SSRI does not work, then best practice is to try a different SSRI in the highest dose you can manage for at least 12 (preferably 16) weeks. If you have tried two or three SSRIs at the highest dose you can manage and for at least 12 weeks, but your symptoms are not improving, then the advice would be to try clomipramine.

Clomipramine is an older drug in a class called a 'tricyclic' which was first used for the treatment of depression, and was found to help OCD in the 1960s. It is not strictly classified as an SSRI because although it has an effect on serotonin receptors, it also enhances other chemicals. This means that it causes more side effects. As with other anti-obsessional drugs, the benefits of the medication will depend on the dose. This means that for many people the higher the dose, the greater the drug's effect in reducing obsessional symptoms. However, higher doses also lead to more side effects. These can be irritating but include dry mouth, constipation, dizziness, tremor, drowsiness and all the side effects discussed above. Most of the side effects are related to the dose and tend to reduce over time, but some may not. They will go away if you stop taking the drug.

Stopping an SSRI or clomipramine

When you stop taking an SSRI or clomipramine, you may experience symptoms for a few days or weeks. These can include dizziness, problems sleeping, agitation or anxiety, nausea, excessive sweating and numbness. These are not the same as the withdrawal symptoms that can occur with minor tranquilizers (drugs of dependence). These symptoms of rebound anxiety caused by tranquilizers may last for many months. It is, however, sensible to reduce SSRIs gradually over several weeks when you do stop taking one. This will also help to reduce the risk of relapse. If the symptoms continue when the lower dose range of the drug is reached, then it may be a good idea to halve it before stopping it completely.

How long do I need to take medication for?

Relapse in OCD is common when you stop taking medication *and* especially if you have had no cognitive behaviour therapy. If relapse does occur, then it usually does so within two to four months of stopping an SSRI. The risk of relapse will partly depend on the natural pattern of OCD without treatment.

So, the advice is usually to remain on medication for at least one to two years after recovery. It depends a lot on individual circumstances. If you are planning to stop medication, it is best to do it after talking to your doctor and within an agreed time frame. Be aware that your OCD symptoms may start to return within a few months. The tricky problem is that if you stop the medication and then start it again you may not recover to your previous state. You might want to start the same SSRI that helped in the past but you may now find that you no longer respond to it or that you need a higher dose to see the same benefit as before.

If CBT has been unavailable or unsuccessful then you may need to take medication in the long term. As SSRIs have been taken for many years without any serious side effects, experts regard this as quite safe.

There is no evidence that any other psychiatric medication is of any benefit in emetophobia. We do *not* recommend tranquilizers like diazepam, lorazepam or alprazolam, or a newer drug pregabalin, for emetophobia. They may reduce your anxiety and nausea *in the short term*. In higher doses, they make it more difficult to learn to tolerate anxiety. They are also addictive in the long term and only prescribed for emergencies. They can become another safety-seeking behaviour. If you have been taking them regularly, then stopping will need to be managed carefully and slowly to minimize possible withdrawal symptoms.

Chapter summary

- Anti-nausea drugs are a safety-seeking behaviour and treatment is likely to involve stopping taking these.
- Although no drug is licensed for use in emetophobia, evidence suggests that SSRIs are helpful in OCD when it is similar to emetophobia.
- SSRIs may take some time to work, and so it is recommended to take the medication for 12 weeks at the largest dose you can manage before judging if symptoms have improved.
- SSRIs can cause side effects, and many of these will improve as your body gets used to the drug.
- Any side effects that do not get better can be helped by halving the dose, and then gradually building up to the target dose.
- If side effects are too hard to live with, then a different SSRI might be recommended.
- All medication use – and especially stopping medication – should be discussed with and managed by your doctor.

CHAPTER 9

——

Considering your Support Network

For people with emetophobia, deciding to start a course of therapy – either through self-help with this book, or by other means – can be a difficult (yet important) step. Before you begin, it can be helpful to consider your support network and to use this throughout your recovery journey. Having a sympathetic ear to listen or someone to talk through any difficulties with can be important factors in staying on track with your goals. In our experience, making changes can be hard and you might find you have periods of up and down. You may experience setbacks, which are very common. Therefore, having people around you whom you trust and can talk to openly can make all the difference. We will now consider common difficulties in finding a support network and how you can overcome them.

Lack of understanding from others

'Well, no one likes being sick.' Emetophobia can make people feel very alone. Yes, it is true that vomiting is not a nice experience for most people, but having emetophobia is far from just a 'dislike' of vomiting. It can be very upsetting when people around you do not understand how hard your phobia is and the huge impact it can have on your life. This is likely to make you feel isolated from others, and alone. However, it is important to remember that you are not alone with your emetophobia. There are many people who share the same fears and are going through the same problems. It can be helpful to calmly explain to others the types of thoughts, feelings and behaviours that you are experiencing. It can also help to explain that although they may never had heard of emetophobia, it is reasonably well recognized by health professionals and there are effective treatments available. It is, in fact, the most common type of specific phobia that people seek help for. It is true that some health professionals may be dismissive or lack experience in emetophobia. It may be helpful to prepare a few responses to have up your sleeve, just in case you need to explain to people who do not understand. Focus on the impact it has on your life and how it is a recognized phobia. It is best to do this when you are feeling calm and emotionally well. It can be much harder to respond in a helpful way when you are feeling upset or anxious.

In our experience, most people will want to support you and to learn more about what you are going through. If they need educating about emetophobia, then who better to help them understand more about it than you? Maybe lend them this book! However, you may find a very small proportion of people still do not understand and may not be in a position to be supportive. In these cases, it may be best to think carefully (if possible) about whether they are the type of people that you need in your life at this time. We will now consider the sources of support that could be available to you. For many people, surrounding themselves with people that they trust and that understand can be valuable in overcoming emetophobia.

Friends and family

Opening up to close family and friends can feel like a difficult first step. You might never have spoken about your difficulties to anyone before. You might feel deeply ashamed about them. Many people worry about telling others about their emetophobia, and here are some common concerns:

- Others making judgements about you.
- Others thinking about or treating you differently.
- People telling others about your difficulties.
- Showing emotion to others and this feeling uncomfortable.
- Making other people very worried about you, or feeling like a 'burden'.
- People making you feel as if your problem is 'not that bad' or that you are overreacting.

These are all very understandable concerns that can make talking to others hard. For many people, however, close friends and family are able to provide emotional support for emetophobia. It can feel like a big sense of relief to finally talk to someone you're close to and help them understand your difficulties. Many find that a problem shared starts to feel smaller, and easier to overcome. It can be helpful to think about how you might respond to a close friend or family member if they were going through a hard time. How might you feel or respond to these same concerns about you? Often people report that many of these fears did not come true and opening up is a positive experience.

It is important here to talk about the difference between *emotional support* and *reassurance seeking*. As we discussed in Chapter 2, seeking reassurance from close family and friends can be unhelpful and keep your fear going. It can be very hard for these loved ones not to reassure you when you are upset, as they believe they are being helpful. People can therefore get into unhelpful patterns of reassurance seeking with loved ones, as they know they are likely to get the reassurance they want. If you think this might be happening to you, it is important to talk to the person who is giving you reassurance. Explain how it is unhelpful for you. You can then agree with this person how you would like to be supported when you are tempted to seek reassurance. It is likely that your anxiety might not like a different response, so it is especially important that you both agree on this *before you become anxious*. You might agree that a loved one provides *emotional support* instead, such as a listening ear, a hug, holding your hand or making you a cup of tea, rather than reassurance about whether they feel ill or you look pale and so on. This is likely to work best if you are specific about what both of you can expect from the interaction, and then agree to stick to it no matter what happens!

Friends and family can provide support alongside any treatment you receive for your emetophobia. They can act as a 'co-therapist' or a 'champion' in your recovery journey. You may find it helpful to show them the work you have done, especially the 'vicious flower model' and the factors that are keeping your phobia going. If they are aware of these, then it is more likely that they can help you to make long-lasting changes. They may be able to add important information about your behaviours that you have not thought of yourself. Close friends and family are in a good position to do this as the people who know you best. They can play an important part in helping you stay on track and not allowing the emetophobia to thrive and go about unchecked. Finally, they may be helpful in supporting any decisions around whether or when to seek professional help for your emetophobia. We would recommend that they read Chapter 10, which includes advice and information for loved ones of adults and young people with emetophobia.

What if they don't understand or are not supportive?

It can be very hard if you don't get the response you hoped for when opening up about your difficulties to friends and family. This might happen if parents or loved ones feel as though your difficulties are their fault. If this happens, it might help to explain to them that it is no one's fault that you have this problem, that there are good treatment options out there and there is hope you can get better. If emotions do get high, this is understandable, and it can be helpful to revisit the conversation at a better time when everyone is feeling calm.

Having space to reflect on these issues with others who are supportive can be a good source of help. It is also okay to explain to others how you need to be supported with your emetophobia if they find it hard to know what to say or do. Ultimately, the decision to involve loved ones in your journey is up to you and it is okay to find support by any means as long as it is the right support for you.

Work and education

Many people choose not to talk about their mental health difficulties to people at work or school. This is a personal choice, and it is very understandable if this is what you decide. However, it can be helpful to understand your rights in relation to mental health, as there are laws that protect you. The Equality Act 2010 is a law passed in the United Kingdom with the main aim of protecting the rights of all people so that everyone has the same chances in life. If you live elsewhere there are likely to be similar laws. In the workplace and public services such as schools and colleges, this act states that it is illegal to treat people with a certain characteristic differently without a good reason. These characteristics include gender, age, race, disability and sexual orientation. The act states that mental health problems are a disability if they affect a person's ability to carry out day-to-day tasks in the long term. The Equality Act therefore states that employers and education providers cannot discriminate unfairly against you if you have a disability. Employers cannot ask medical questions relating to your mental health before offering you a job. Employers and education providers must also protect you from harassment or victimization, and make changes to help you to do your job or to learn if it is reasonable for them to do so. If you have been treated unfairly because of your mental health, you can take legal action.

This information might not change how you feel about talking about your emetophobia at work, school or college. However, it can be helpful to talk to a supportive manager or a teacher about your difficulties so that they can support you to do your best. Others can find talking to close colleagues or peers helpful as an extra source of emotional support. If you decide to do this, it is important to understand your rights so that you are still treated fairly. For more information about the Equality Act in the UK and how it may be relevant to you, visit www.gov.uk/guidance/equality-act-2010-guidance. Similar legislation may exist around the world.

Professional help

When to consider getting professional help

For some people, reading a self-help book for their problems may be enough to learn the tools and skills needed to overcome them. For others, more intensive support might be needed to get better from their phobia and live their lives in line with their values and goals. This does not mean that those people are not motivated, and it is not their fault. We know that, for many people, emetophobia can develop very early on and it can be more difficult to treat than other phobias. The longer a person has experienced a problem, generally the more support they are likely to need. That is not to say that these cases are without hope, it might just take a bit more help from outside sources. If you have tried to work with this book, and you feel that things are not changing as much as you would like after one month or so, then you should be very proud of yourself for trying self-help first. Be kind to yourself, and instead of blaming yourself or thinking you have failed, try to think of seeking professional help as just the next step of your journey.

Professional help is most likely to involve regular therapy with a trained professional such as a psychologist, psychiatrist, therapist or counsellor. It is likely that moderate to severe anxiety problems will need to be treated by a trained professional. There are many ways to access this type of help in the UK and we will discuss this below.

Types of professional help

Cognitive behavioural therapy is shown to be most effective at treating emetophobia. Other forms of treatment such as psychotherapy, counselling and hypnotherapy are not helpful for emetophobia. Medication plus CBT may be beneficial for more severe cases and when there is OCD, but medication alone is rarely helpful. CBT is typically known as a 'talking and doing' therapy, and to get the most benefit out of it, it requires effort, motivation and work on your part. Often the work that you do outside therapy sessions is the biggest driver of change. If there is a lot going on in your life that will make committing yourself to such a therapy difficult, it might be better to wait until a more suitable time.

If you are already seeing a therapist for your emetophobia and you are not sure what kind of therapy you are having, it is good to ask. Features of 'good CBT' involve the following aspects:

- Structured sessions with a beginning, middle and end and clear goals that you want to achieve.
- Use of the 'vicious flower' or similar model such as Theory A and B to help you have a good understanding of how it is your solutions that are the problem and are making your distress worse.
- A focus on problems in the here and now, rather than in the past and your childhood. Of course, it is helpful to have a good understanding of how the problem developed and any emotional links to the past, but the focus needs to be on the present.
- A focus on skills and tools to help you find solutions to your difficulties. At the heart of this will be learning to tolerate uncertainty, difficult feelings and how to test out your expectations.
- Acknowledgement that the problems you are working on are most important and relevant to you right now.
- Regular homework tasks that help you move towards your goals and values.
- Feeling as if you and your therapist are equal partners and able to work together towards a shared goal.

If you feel unsure that your therapist is offering you any of the above, it might be a good idea to discuss this with them. You have a right to access helpful treatment and should never feel embarrassed or pressured by someone who is helping you. Research shows that one of the biggest helpful factors in therapy is the relationship you have with your therapist. If you feel that you don't 'click' with your current therapist or that they are not meeting your needs, then it is okay to change therapists to someone who can (if it is practical to do so, as it may not always be).

Getting started

The following information is mainly relevant for the UK. Your general practitioner (GP) is often the best person to talk to if you are thinking of seeking professional help. They should know the best options for treatment locally and will be able to make a referral to relevant services on your behalf.

Improving Access to Psychological Therapies (IAPT)

One accessible form of outpatient CBT for emetophobia in the UK can be accessed through your local Improving Access to Psychological Therapies service. This can be found through a search of 'NHS talking therapies' plus your local area. IAPT services aim to provide evidence-based treatments that are accessible by everyone in the community. You can refer yourself online or by phone. You will then be invited to speak to a trained professional confidentially over the phone so that they can understand your difficulties and offer you the right type of treatment. This may involve:

- Guided self-help, where a professional works with you using self-help resources.

- Group therapies, accessed by other people experiencing the same problems.
- Workshops, run by professionals about a variety of general problems such as low mood, stress or worry.
- Individual therapy, usually up to 16 sessions with a trained professional.

Even if you do not take up treatment through a talking therapy service, it can still be helpful to have an assessment with one. They can signpost to relevant services in your local area if they feel other services are more suitable for your difficulties. As such, they are often a good first port of call if you have not received any professional help in the past.

You can also seek a referral from your GP to a specialist outpatient service for emetophobia under 'Patient Choice' at the Centre for Anxiety Disorders and Trauma at the Maudsley Hospital in South London.

Anxiety Disorders Residential Unit

This is a national specialist residential service based at the Bethlem Royal Hospital, in Beckenham, Kent. This unit provides a more intensive programme for people with more severe and long-term anxiety disorders such as emetophobia. You can only be referred by your community mental health team and if you have not made progress in outpatient CBT.

Private therapists

So far, we have discussed ways of accessing therapy through the National Health Service (NHS). These options are free of charge but are likely to involve a wait, and in some cases quite a lengthy wait, depending on need in the area. Another option might be to search for a private therapist if you are in a position to pay for treatment. You will usually be able to start your treatment right away with a private therapist. One downside of private therapy is that it can be less regulated than professionals working for the NHS. This means it can be harder to know if a professional has the right training or experience or is offering the right type of therapy.

One way of finding a CBT accredited therapist is to search on the British Association for Behavioural & Cognitive Psychotherapies (BABCP) website. This is the leading organization for CBT in the UK and Ireland, and as such you can be confident that a BABCP accredited therapist will be delivering CBT to a minimum standard. However, we strongly advise talking to the therapist and finding out about their experience of treating emetophobia. You can search for a therapist by location and check accreditation and experience on the following website: https://cbtregisteruk.com/Default.aspx.

Barriers to accessing therapy and how to overcome them

If you are told you have to wait a long time for therapy

This often varies by location, but NHS services can be in high demand and waiting lists can be lengthy. Once you are on a waiting list, however, you might consider using alternative sources of support to keep you going while you wait. For example, self-help resources might help you to understand your difficulties and how you can be helping them in the meantime. Self-help might better prepare you for therapy once you do reach the top of the waiting list. Further information found in books, articles, support groups or forums may be helpful. If you feel you have been waiting for a while, it is always worth calling the service to check where you are on the waiting list. If you are willing to see a trainee therapist then this can sometimes mean you can access treatment sooner. Trainees are often highly capable and knowledgeable professionals, who are receiving good supervision, so can be a credible source of support.

If you feel ashamed or embarrassed about talking to a therapist

This is a common and understandable feeling when seeking help. It can feel odd talking to a stranger, especially if you have not told many people about your emetophobia before. However, most therapists are trained professionals who have a great deal of experience of working with people with similar difficulties. They have experience of listening to people with mental health problems and are skilled at responding in an empathic and compassionate way. Everything you say to a therapist is treated confidentially and cannot be shared unless there is concern for your safety or the safety of someone else. If you still have concerns, then it might help to raise these with the professional or service that you refer to. They might be able to put you at ease.

If you feel that other people are more deserving of help and you shouldn't 'waste' a professional's time

Everyone deserves to be free of anxiety, and to live a life that is meaningful and valued. No matter how mild or severe your difficulties, you have a right to treatment and no professional should ever make you feel that you are not worthy of their time.

If you feel hopeless or afraid that nothing will change

Feeling hopeless and 'stuck' can be a common feature of emetophobia, especially if you have had it for a long time. You might think that nobody will understand or be able to help you. If you are also feeling depressed this is more likely to be the case. In our experience, talking to a professional and engaging in CBT can be helpful for most people. It is often taking the first step that is the hardest one to achieve. However, once you have taken this and seen some small changes, the motivation usually takes over and you will start to feel more hopeful.

What if I feel hopeless and want to end my life?

If you are really struggling with your emetophobia, you might feel very hopeless and have thoughts to end your life. These are very understandable when difficulties seem overwhelming but can be very frightening. If this happens, it is important to seek help *immediately – do not wait.* Here are some sources of support if you are worried that you cannot keep yourself safe:

- Call your GP practice or the out-of-hours number if it is closed – you should find this on the practice website.
- Call the Samaritans, a 24-hour confidential listening service, on 116 123.
- If you have a community team, call your care co-ordinator or their crisis number.
- If you are very worried and have limited options for support, go straight to your local A&E department for immediate help.

Support groups and charities

Further sources of support for emetophobia can be accessed through charities, websites and social media. The following is a list that we have put together of the ones that we know about, although you may come across others that we have not included.

Charities

The only dedicated charity for emetophobia is Emetophobia Action. It is very new but aims to provide information and advice to people with emetophobia and their families; increase public awareness and provide education about emetophobia; advance research into emetophobia; and assist those treating emetophobia by promoting best practice. We are both trustees of this new charity and are very keen for donations or fundraising for the charity to help support the community of people with emetophobia internationally.

Emetophobia Action
Website: www.emetaction.org
Email: info@emetaction.org
Donate at: www.givey.com/emetophobiaaction

Various other UK-based charities exist for other anxiety disorders, which may offer help and support for emetophobia. These include:

Anxiety UK
Helpline: 03444 775 774
Website: www.anxietyuk.org.uk
Email: support@anxietyuk.org.uk

OCD Action
Helpline: 0845 390 6232
Website: www.ocdaction.org.uk
Email: support@ocdaction.org.uk

OCD-UK

Support queries: 03332 127 890

Website: www.ocduk.org

Email: admin@ocduk.org

USA

Anxiety and Depression Association of America

Website: https://adaa.org

Email: information@adaa.org

Websites and bulletin boards

There are several free online resources for people with emetophobia. Often people find bulletin boards helpful when they first meet other people with emetophobia, but in the long term it may be unhelpful if they keep searching for reassurance or for advice about norovirus or better ways of avoiding. It is therefore important to be mindful of this when using the following resources.

Bulletin board at International Emetophobia Society:
www.emetophobia.org

Frequently Asked Questions page:
https://emetophobia.scienceontheweb.net

Vomit Phobia:
www.vphobia.com

Emetophobia Help:
https://emetophobiahelp.org

Books

Living with Emetophobia: Coping with Extreme Fear of Vomiting by Nicolette Heaton-Harris, London: Jessica Kingsley Publishers, 2007

Social media

Facebook
Emetophobia Help:
www.facebook.com/EmetophobiaHelp

Emetophobia Help and Support:
www.facebook.com/groups/412853615474996

Emetophobia support group:
www.facebook.com/groups/732242036808794

Instagram
The Emetophobia Review – movies/TV shows involving triggers:
www.instagram.com/emetophobiareview/?hl=en

Chapter summary

- A good support network can be very helpful in overcoming your emetophobia.
- Opening up to friends and family about your emetophobia can feel daunting; however, sometimes they can offer valuable support alongside treatment.
- Talking to your manager or colleagues at work may not be necessary but can be useful to see if any extra supports can be put in place, and it is helpful here to know your rights about mental health in the workplace.
- There are many ways to seek professional help in the UK if self-help is not enough for you at this time.
- A good place to start is either your local IAPT service or talking to your GP.
- Charities, support groups, websites and social media can all be helpful sources of additional support.

———

CHAPTER 10

Advice for Friends, Partners and Family Members

This chapter is addressed to people who live with or are supporting either adults or young people who have emetophobia. Any chapters of this book will be useful for carers to read; however, this chapter summarizes the most helpful points for the loved ones of those trying to overcome their emetophobia.

Offering support as a 'co-therapist'

As a friend, partner or family member of a person with emetophobia, you are in a unique position to offer them support. If they have chosen to confide in you about their difficulties, it is likely that they trust you and your ability to meet their emotional needs. It is often hard for someone with emetophobia to open up. They may be afraid that others will judge them or think that their phobia is trivial. Above all, it is important that the person feels understood. It is helpful to give the message that their feelings are valid and understandable given the experiences they have had. We know that overcoming emetophobia – either by self-help or therapy – is a difficult journey that can be full of ups and downs. There will be times that your loved one may not believe they can do it and may think about giving up.

Any treatment is more likely to be successful with the support of loved ones. As a friend, partner or family member you can help by acting as your loved one's 'co-therapist'. This role involves understanding the processes of change and supporting your loved one to commit to them. It is about providing emotional support, encouragement and the motivation to continue, even on their worst days. You may decide to read through this book together, or your loved one may share only parts of it with you. This is entirely up to you. In our experience, a co-therapist is most helpful when they are patient, encouraging, understanding, able to contain their loved one's distress and tell them that they can bear it.

Understanding maintenance factors and supporting change

We recommend that you read Chapter 2 of this book as a minimum. This outlines the main features of emetophobia that you are likely to recognize in your loved one. As a carer, it is important that you are familiar with these and how they keep anxiety going. Your loved one will have to find the courage to make changes to their thought patterns and behaviours. They must be brave enough to face their fears, and to do that they may need your help. It will also be important for you to know some of the processes that are going on, so you can make sure you do not become part of the problem yourself by allowing the emetophobia to remain unchallenged.

Avoidance

When your loved one is feeling anxious, it is very common that they will avoid certain activities or situations. This helps them to feel less anxious! However, the more they avoid things, the less they will learn about the real risks of vomiting and what it is actually like. Therefore, over time they will become more afraid of it.

The experience of emetophobia is unique to each person, and you may already have a good sense of what your loved one avoids. Typically, it is certain foods or restaurants; crowded places like public transport or busy environments; people who are more likely to vomit such as drunk or sick people, or children; travelling abroad; hospitals; or activities that might make them feel sick such as fairground rides or travel by boat. You may find that your loved one is avoiding work, college or school for fear of being sick.

It can be very challenging for a carer to understand and deal with avoidance. After all, this is likely to affect you too! As a carer, the best way to support someone to reverse avoidance and face their fears is to encourage them *at their own pace*. Remember, the things they are avoiding may not be scary to you, but to someone with emetophobia they can be incredibly challenging. The longer things have been avoided, the harder it will be to face them again. So your loved one will benefit from patience, encouragement and understanding. If things go well, celebrate each small win with them. If not, don't criticize or nag. Try to avoid saying things like 'It's really not that bad' or 'Just get on with it'. This is likely to make them feel worse.

It is important for the person with emetophobia to create opportunities to learn alternative ways of thinking about vomiting themselves, as it will be very hard for them to take your word for it. Take the time to understand why it was not possible to face something this time and make a plan together to try again. Maybe your loved one was trying to attempt too much too soon. Can you go back and make a plan that is more realistic? If your loved one is beating themselves up, it may be your job to support them to be kinder to themselves. Remind them that change can be hard and they are doing a good job by trying. Even if you don't feel it yourself, keeping your loved one hopeful for a future without emetophobia will be helpful.

Safety-seeking behaviours

These are things that people with emetophobia do in situations that make them anxious, but they cannot avoid. It might be behaviours that reduce feelings of nausea, or the possibility of vomiting. It is likely to make them feel less anxious in the short term; however, these behaviours will keep anxiety going over time. They prevent opportunities to learn that vomiting is not likely or as bad as they think.

Typical safety-seeking behaviours in emetophobia include excessive hand washing or cleaning, overcooking food, checking expiry dates of food, chewing mints or gum, taking regular sips of water, using anti-nausea medication, and mental activities such as repeating certain words or phrases in their head. To overcome emetophobia, it is important that safety-seeking behaviours are stopped entirely. As a carer, it will be helpful for you to recognize when your loved one is using safety-seeking behaviours, and to gently encourage them to stop. A gentle and understanding approach to this is more likely to be successful than criticism, nagging or bullying. Remember that to someone with emetophobia, these behaviours may be the only thing saving them from the worst thing happening to them. Therefore, it is very normal that people struggle to stop using them. They may not even be aware that they are doing it if it is a behaviour that started a long time ago. Your role here may be to help increase your loved one's awareness of their unhelpful behaviours, and to remind them why it is important to stop using them. Perhaps you could decide together the best way to go about this, to ensure that you are both on the same page and that your support is most likely to be helpful. You might agree on the most problematic or frequent behaviours, and exactly what your loved one would like you to say or do to help them to stop using them. Regardless of how you decide to do this, it is important that you take a united approach to avoid conflict or resistance to your efforts to help.

Alternatives to reassurance

In Chapter 2, we learned that reassurance seeking may keep emetophobia going. When your loved one feels anxious, it is very natural that they might ask you if things are going to be okay, check that you feel well or that the risk of vomiting is low in various situations. This makes sense to them, as in the short term it helps to manage their anxiety. However, over time, excessive reassurance seeking serves to keep the anxiety high as it reinforces the message that there is something to be afraid of. It sends the message that reassurance is needed, because the threat of vomiting is real and if it happens it will be awful. This keeps your loved one attuned to threat, which makes them more anxious in the long run.

Therefore, it is important that you do not fall into the trap of providing reassurance when your loved one seeks it. Instead, you can offer emotional support if they are feeling anxious. This might involve offering them time to sit and listen to how they feel, you might hold their hand or give them a hug. You could offer to make them a cup of tea, run them a bath or suggest going for a walk together. At every step, you are with them and supporting them. You are giving them the message that it is normal and okay to feel the way they feel. However, you are not providing reassurance in relation to questions around vomiting, illness or contamination. For this to be helpful to your loved one, it may be best to agree between you how they would like you to comfort them *before they feel anxious*. This way you will both know what to expect, and this will help you to meet the needs of your loved one and avoid confrontation. Once they become anxious, they may find it harder to stick to the agreement, as the anxiety will be telling them that they must seek reassurance! So be patient with them, try not to get frustrated, remind them calmly what you agreed together and stick to it.

Advice for parents and carers of young people with emetophobia

Emetophobia typically begins earlier than other phobias, and it can affect children as well as adults. Children are particularly vulnerable to developing emetophobia if they experience or witness a traumatic episode of vomiting at a young age. However, this is not to say that every child who vomits will go on to develop a phobia as it is usually caused by a combination of factors. Emetophobia may be harder to spot in younger people, as it may not be obvious initially. It may take several more years to fully see the impact of avoidance and safety-seeking behaviours on their lives. It may be the first signs of other problems such as OCD-type behaviours. It can be harder to engage children in treatment, and certainly the longer these difficulties go untreated, the harder they will be to overcome. Therefore, as parents or family members, it is important to familiarize yourself with the common features of emetophobia so you can be aware and spot it early.

One common difficulty in supporting children is that they can find it harder to recognize and label their emotions. This might mean that they are more likely to report physical symptoms such as tummy ache or pain instead of anxiety. This might lead to a young person being seen by a medical doctor rather than a mental health professional. Emetophobia may be misdiagnosed as something else entirely. It can be helpful to use visual cues such as faces to label emotions, or an anxiety thermometer to measure levels of anxiety in any situation. This is typically a visual representation of a thermometer that signifies different levels in intensity of an emotion. For younger people, it is less likely they will know what emetophobia is, or that other people have the same condition. They may lack access to resources such as the internet or books to read about their difficulties. Therefore, they might believe that they are the only one to have the phobia or that their feelings are stupid. This might make it harder for them to open up to others about it. It is important here to help the child to feel safe in sharing their difficulties, and that their feelings are always valid no matter what they are.

As parents or family members, it is important to not become part of the problem by supporting your child to engage in unhelpful behaviours. It might be harder to engage young people in facing their fears or letting go of unhelpful behaviours that make them feel safe. You may find that your child is avoiding school or other important activities. In this case, it is important to gently encourage your child to face their fears so that they can learn a more positive way to think about vomiting. Here you will need to strike the right balance between trying to understand their fears and being supportive, while encouraging them to attend. Try to avoid getting frustrated with them, as this can make things worse. Instead, stay calm and try to understand exactly what your child is most afraid of and make a plan together about how you can support them to overcome this.

If you are worried about your child's well-being, talk to your family GP. It may be important that they access services as early as possible if professional help is required.

Looking after yourself

If your loved one is suffering, it is common to worry and feel responsible for them. You might want to try and help them as much as you possibly can. It is normal to have feelings of anxiety, helplessness, guilt or hopelessness yourself when caring for a loved one with emetophobia. You may find that the difficulties of your loved one impact on your well-being too. It is important to look after yourself as well as your loved one. The caring role can be emotionally and physically demanding, and you need to take time to rest yourself. This is important, as taking time for yourself means that you are better able to care for others. What can you do to be kind to yourself? Perhaps taking some time to relax, doing something you enjoy or talking to someone about how you feel might be helpful.

Chapter summary

- Acting as a 'co-therapist' can be a helpful source of support to someone trying to overcome their emetophobia.
- It is important to familiarize yourself with common processes that keep it going, so that you don't become part of the problem!
- Encourage your loved one to face their fears and drop their unhelpful behaviours.
- Offer emotional support instead of reassurance.
- A kind, patient and gentle approach is more likely to be effective, especially with children and young people.
- Prioritize looking after yourself as well as your loved one.

About the Authors

Alexandra Keyes is a clinical psychologist and BABCP accredited cognitive behavioural psychotherapist, offering evidence-based CBT to both NHS and private patients. She works at a national specialist residential unit for people with severe and enduring anxiety disorders at the South London and Maudsley NHS Foundation Trust. She completed her doctoral research investigating time intensive cognitive behavioural therapies and imagery re-scripting in emetophobia. She has published scientific papers on the subject of emetophobia and is passionate about raising awareness and improving accessible treatments for those who have the condition. She is a trustee of Emetophobia Action, the national charity for emetophobia.

David Veale is a consultant psychiatrist in cognitive behavioural psychotherapies and leads a national outpatient and residential unit service for people with severe treatment refractory anxiety disorders at the South London and Maudsley Trust (www.veale.co.uk). He is a Visiting Professor at the Institute of Psychiatry, Psychology and Neuroscience, King's College London. He has been researching emetophobia since 2005 and has published 11 scientific papers on the topic. He was a member of the group that wrote the NICE guidelines on OCD in 2006 and chaired the NICE Evidence Update on OCD in 2013. He is an Honorary Fellow of the British Association of Behavioural and Cognitive Psychotherapies, a Fellow of the British Psychological Society and a Fellow of the Royal College of Psychiatrists. He is a trustee of the national charities Emetophobia Action, OCD Action and the Body Dysmorphic Disorder Foundation.

Index